WHO AND WHEN?

The 20th CENTURY: Pre-1945

Artists, Writers, and Composers

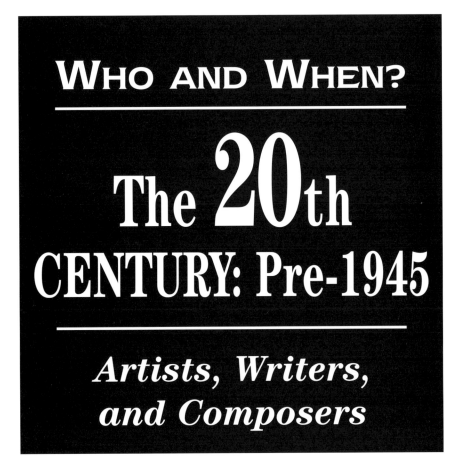

WHO AND WHEN?

The 20th CENTURY: Pre-1945

Artists, Writers, and Composers

Edited by Sarah Halliwell

RSVP
RAINTREE
STECK-VAUGHN
PUBLISHERS
The Steck-Vaughn Company

Austin, Texas

Steck-Vaughn Company

First published 1998 by Raintree Steck-Vaughn Publishers,
an imprint of Steck-Vaughn Company.
Copyright © 1998 Marshall Cavendish Limited.

Library of Congress Cataloging-in-Publication Data
20th century: pre-1945: artists, writers, and composers / edited by Sarah Halliwell
p. cm. -- (Who and When; v. 7)
Includes bibliographical references and index.
Summary: Introduces some of the major artists, writers, and composers that flourished
in Europe and the United States during the first half of the twentieth century.
ISBN 0-8172-4731-9
1. Artists -- Biography -- Juvenile literature. 2. Arts, Modern -- 20th century -- Juvenile literature. [1. Arts, Modern -- 20th century. 2. Artists. 3. Authors. 4. Composers.]
I. Halliwell, Sarah. II. Title: Twentieth Century (1900-1945). III. Series.
NX456.A14 1998
700'.92'2--dc21   97-30957
[B]   CIP
                                                                                              AC

Printed and bound in Italy
1 2 3 4 5 6 7 8 9 0 LE 02 01 00 99 98 97

Marshall Cavendish Limited
Managing Editor: Ellen Dupont
Project Editor: Sarah Halliwell
Senior Editor: Andrew Brown
Senior Designer: Richard Newport
Designer: Richard Shiner
Picture administrator: Vimu Patel
Production: Craig Chubb
Index: Susan Bosanko

Raintree Steck-Vaughn
Publishing Director: Walter Kossmann
Project Manager: Joyce Spicer
Editor: Shirley Shalit

Consultants:
Colin Wiggins, National Gallery, London;
Sean Francis, University of Chicago;
Jonathan Kulp, University of Texas.

Contributors:
Iain Zaczek, Lorien Kite,
Andrew Brown.

CONTENTS

INTRODUCTION

At the dawn of the new century, crowds flocked to Europe's largest celebration, the World's Fair in Paris. There, they gazed in wonder at exhibits of progress, such as the Palace of Electricity, and marveled at the exotic displays from every part of the globe. The coming years, it seemed, were full of promise.

Some of this optimism was justified. The Western nations had never been richer, with valuable colonial possessions spread throughout Africa and Asia. The United States had also entered the imperial race, with the acquisition of Puerto Rico, Guam, and the Philippines. Technology, too, was advancing at a spectacular rate. In 1903, the Wright brothers made their famous airplane flight at Kittyhawk and, in the same year, Henry Ford founded the Ford Motor Company in Detroit, ushering in an age of mass production. It was also an age of communication, with exciting new developments such as the radio and movies.

The art scene of the early 1900s was incredibly rich. For painters, the development of photography meant that there was less concern with simply copying nature. Instead, artists tried to find new ways of capturing the changing world around them. Their discoveries shattered traditional ideas about art. The Cubists, led by Pablo Picasso (*see page 26*), broke objects down into geometric shapes; the Fauves, such as Henri Matisse (*see page 12*), employed bright, unrealistic colors; while the Expressionists gave their pictures emotional intensity by distorting reality. All these movements were steps toward abstract art—art that expresses an idea or feeling rather than recognizable objects—which Wassily Kandinsky pioneered in 1910.

Composers were experimenting along similar lines, sacrificing harmony and melody in their search for something new. The results sounded so chaotic that many listeners were baffled: The first performance of Igor Stravinsky's (*see page 80*) ballet, *The Rite of Spring*, for example, almost caused a riot. In Europe, the key figures were Stravinsky and Alfred Schoenberg: At the same time in the United States, Aaron Copland (*see page 88*) and Charles Ives (*see page 76*) brought new life to music.

But this period of productivity would soon end. The political stability that created these benefits was dangerously fragile. Peace in Europe depended on a complex network of alliances—and in 1914, the entire system came crashing down, with the outbreak of World War I. Though centered on Europe, the war affected countries all around the globe, including the United States, which joined the Allied fight against Germany in 1917. The conflict was one of unprecedented carnage: More than ten million people were killed and twice as many wounded during four devastating years.

In the United States, the end of the war marked the beginning of a period of optimism known as the "Jazz Age." The name pays tribute to the growing importance of black culture. Ragtime, blues, and jazz had all made their mark on popular music and, in the 1920s, both George Gershwin (*see page 84*) and Copland combined jazz rhythms with classical forms. The rhythms of jazz also inspired artist Piet Mondrian (*see page 18*), who translated them into abstract paintings. The era's chief spokesman, F. Scott Fitzgerald (*see page 56*), captured the high spirits and fast living in both his novels and his life. At the same time, African American artists and writers such as Zora Neale Hurston (*see page 68*) led the Harlem Renaissance.

In 1929, the Wall Street crash—the collapse of the stock market—brought an abrupt end to the exuberance of the Jazz Age, marking the start of the Great Depression. This bleak era saw widespread unemployment and poverty. Yet the rise of American literature continued. The poor and the downtrodden struggled to survive in John Steinbeck's (*see page 72*) novels, while Eugene O'Neill (*see page 52*) enhanced his reputation as the father of American theater. Many American writers celebrated the American landscape. Robert Frost's (*see page 40*) verses sang of the glories of rural New England, while William Faulkner's (*see page 60*) brooding novels painted a vivid picture of the Deep South. In Mexico, Frida Kahlo (*see page 36*) used bold colors and imagery to create a distinctively Mexican art. Her husband, Diego Rivera (*see page 32*), meanwhile, painted rich murals glorifying labor and technology.

In Europe, postwar bitterness and economic hardship aided the spread of fascism, and this extreme right-wing party gained control of Germany and Italy. Its first test of strength came in the Spanish Civil War, between 1936-39. Writers and artists flocked to the republican cause—which inspired Ernest Hemingway's (*see page 64*) *For Whom the Bell Tolls*, and Picasso's *Guernica*—but the Western democracies failed to see the threat. This allowed Adolf Hitler to lead Germany into World War II between 1939-45—the most deadly and destructive conflict in history.

WASSILY KANDINSKY

The first artist to consciously reject the object in his art, Kandinsky faced criticism and ridicule during his lifetime for his abstract painting. Yet his art and his writings altered the course of modern art.

Wassily Kandinsky was born on December 4, 1866, in Moscow, Russia, where his father was a wealthy tea merchant. In 1871, the family moved to the Ukraine, on the Black Sea. His parents divorced soon after.

Despite showing both musical and artistic talent, the young Kandinsky decided on the more acceptable profession of law. At Moscow University from 1886, he proved to be a very bright student. After graduating in 1892, he immediately gained a teaching appointment at the Moscow Law School. Yet he always felt that he would find more fulfillment in art than in his law studies.

COMMITTED TO ART

In 1895, Kandinsky saw an exhibit of the French Impressionists in Moscow. He was stunned by this exciting and colorful new style of painting. Inspired, Kandinsky made a vital decision the following year—to commit himself completely to painting. In 1896, he also married his cousin, Anja Chimiakin.

He set off to Munich, Germany, then a thriving artistic center. "The drudgery is behind me," he declared, "before me lies the kind of work I like." He entered the Anton Azbé art school, then the most popular in Munich. But he found the teaching boring, and often skipped classes. Instead, he decided to try the art classes at the Munich Royal Academy. There, he shocked teachers with his bold colors and exaggerated effects.

Many of his friends described Kandinsky as a quiet and serious man. Even his studio was different from that of most painters—it was neat and tidy, with paints lined up in rows. He was always immaculately clean, and joked that he could paint in evening dress.

In 1902, Kandinsky met the painter Gabriele Münter, who became his pupil. After the breakdown of his marriage, she became his mistress. The couple spent months at a time touring the

The Boat Ride, 1910, by Gabriele Münter **Kandinsky's pupil shows the artist in the year he painted his first abstract work.**

Improvisation Ravine, July 1914, by Wassily Kandinsky
This lively painting dances with dazzling color. It is not entirely abstract—there are still suggestions of a landscape, including mountains, water, ships, and billowing sails.

world, visiting Italy, Switzerland, and even Africa.

Kandinsky's allowance meant that he had no urgent need to sell his work, and so was free to experiment. He was also able to travel, studying the work of the world's avant-garde artists—those developing new or experimental artistic ideas. Inspired by the Fauves—a group of artists who used bold color and distorted shapes—he began painting landscapes in broad masses of color. These works marked a breakthrough in his style. Increasingly, he concentrated on using paint to express feelings and emotions, rather than to represent objects.

In 1910, Kandinsky took this approach further—and made one of the most important developments in the history of art. The artist discovered the value of abstract art—art which does not depict a recognizable object—by accident. One evening, he entered his studio and saw a stunningly beautiful image. He then realized that it was one of his own paintings standing on its side. At that moment, he understood that the realistic depiction of objects was no longer important in his art.

CRITICISM AND RIDICULE

Kandinsky painted his first completely abstract painting in 1910. Critics and the public were horrified. In 1911, he went on to found a new artistic group called *Der Blaue Reiter*—The Blue Rider— with the German painter Franz Marc. This organization was dedicated to a variety of exciting artistic styles, including abstract painting.

Attacks on Kandinsky's work continued. When some of his *Improvisations* paintings were shown in Paris in 1912, a reviewer declared that the works looked as if a dog had dipped its feet or its tail, or both, in a palette, and walked across the canvas. In response, Kandinsky explained his theories in the influential book, *On the Spiritual in Art*.

In 1914, with the outbreak of World War I, Kandinsky left Germany for Russia. In 1917, the Russian Revolution tore the country apart, and over the next years, Kandinsky suffered poverty and hardship. Life was brightened only by his marriage to Nina de Andreewsky.

During this dark period, Kandinsky produced few paintings. He returned to Germany in 1921, depressed and penniless. But in 1922, the artist Paul Klee (*see page 22*) found him a job teaching art at the Bauhaus, a new school which promoted the unification of crafts with functional design. Kandinsky began to experiment with the basic elements of the circle, the triangle, and the square. He published his observations in his 1926 book *Point and Line to Plane*.

Kandinsky's new interest in geometry marked a turning point in his career. But in 1933, the Nazis closed the Bauhaus down, and the artist moved to Neuilly, near Paris. With this move came the final change in Kandinsky's style. He created a whole new group of forms. Strange, amoebalike shapes float in bright background colors.

The artist became more and more solitary, but he was still painting boldly. Throughout a five-year illness, he planned new works. But on December 13, 1944, Kandinsky died. He was 78.

MAJOR WORKS

1910	COMPOSITION NO. 2; SKETCH FOR COMPOSITION IV
1912	ON THE SPIRITUAL IN ART
1913	IMPROVISATION NO. 31
1923	COMPOSITION VIII
1940	SKY BLUE

HENRI MATISSE

One of the most innovative artists of the 20th century, Matisse's experiments in dazzling, intense color marked a turning point in the history of art. His vivid paintings and "cut-outs" express happiness and harmony.

Henri Émile Benoit Matisse was born on December 31, 1869, in Le Cateau, northern France. Soon after, the family moved to the nearby village of Bohain-en-Vermandois, where his father, Émile, set up shop as a druggist and grain merchant. His mother, Anna, was a milliner, or hatmaker.

A PASSIONATE PAINTER

Henri was a sensitive and intelligent boy who did well at school. At the age of 17, he went to study law in Paris. Two years later, Henri started attending early morning drawing classes before beginning his day's work as a lawyer's clerk. In 1890, while he was recovering from an operation, he developed a serious passion for art.

His father was unhappy at the idea of his son giving up the respectable profession of law in order to paint, but eventually gave his permission for Henri to become a full-time art student. The 23-year-old's first teacher was Adolphe William Bouguereau, one of the most successful academic painters of the day. Henri did not like Bouguereau's strict, academic approach, however, so in 1892, he found a new teacher, Gustave Moreau. Moreau was a popular instructor at the School of Fine Arts, the most important art academy in France.

Moreau was an imaginative teacher who encouraged his students to develop their personal talents. He urged Matisse not only to copy Old Masters in the Louvre—the traditional way of learning to paint—but also to go out into the streets and draw, taking his subjects from everyday life.

In 1896, at the age of 26, Matisse had his first artistic success when the Paris Salon exhibited four of his pictures. At this time, his paintings were mainly dark, rather gloomy still lifes and landscapes. Two years later, in 1898, Matisse married Amélie Parayre, a milliner. Over

Henri Matisse, 1954
This photograph, taken on October 4, 1954, was the last of the artist before his death.

the next two years, they had two children—Jean and Pierre.

By this time, Matisse's style had changed considerably. Under the influence of the Postimpressionists, who built up their paintings with dots, patches, and blocks of intense color, he had discovered the joy of color. In June 1904, Matisse had his first one-man show. It was not a success, however.

THE "WILD BEASTS"

Later the same year, Matisse changed his style again. He now began using bold, flat areas of even brighter colors. He aimed to "exalt all colors together, sacrificing none of them." A few other artists were beginning to handle color in the same dramatic way, and in the fall of 1905, they exhibited together at the

---

"When I started to paint, I felt transported into a kind of paradise."
(Henri Matisse)

Salon in Paris. Most of the critics mocked their work. One described the artists as *fauves*—"wild beasts"—with Matisse as their king.

Yet this exhibit proved to be a turning point in Matisse's career. Gertrude and Leo Stein, an American brother and sister, bought the most controversial picture, Matisse's *Woman with a Hat.*

KING OF THE WILD BEASTS

Matisse was the leader of a group of artists who burst onto the Paris art scene in 1905, shocking the public.

Matisse and his colleagues—including André Dérain, Georges Braque, Georges Rouault, and Maurice de Vlaminck—used line, color, and pattern to express their feelings. They were inspired by the way in which Postimpressionist artists Vincent van Gogh and Paul Gauguin used color purely for its emotional effects.

Matisse and the others used color with a ferocious new intensity. In particular, they used nonnaturalistic color to create striking effects. They also distorted and flattened their forms. In Matisse's portrait of his wife, for example, he painted a green stripe down the center of her

They went on to buy more of the artist's work, becoming his first major patrons. A year or so later, a rich Russian collector followed the Steins' example. This patronage gave Matisse freedom. It also enabled him to travel, and he visited Germany, Spain, Morocco, and Russia.

The outbreak of World War I in 1914 halted his travels. At the age of 44, Matisse was too old to fight. He painted

face. The picture is made up of flat patches of color (*above*).

This bold new approach sent shock waves through the art world. People were not used to such "savage" colors—colors that clashed and jarred rather than blended and harmonized. Yet the Fauves' experiments with color were highly influential for the future of 20th-century art, liberating artists to use color and form in a highly expressive way.

little for the next few years, concentrating instead on etching, and playing the violin. He joked that this was insurance: if his eyesight failed, and he could not paint, he could play for money.

Although the war slowed Matisse's output, it did not have any dramatic effect on the appearance of his paintings; he was not interested in reflecting the events going on around him. He con-

tinued to be concerned with visual problems. He explained the principle of his work: "What I dream of is an art of balance, of purity, and serenity, devoid of troubling or disturbing subject matter … something like a good armchair in which one rests from physical fatigue."

From 1916 onward, Matisse spent most of his winters on the French Riviera. The dazzling sun and brilliant colors made the South irresistible to an artist for whom color had become of central importance. He painted radiant still lifes, interiors, and female nudes.

INTERNATIONAL SUCCESS

During the 1920s, Matisse began to gain official recognition in France. In 1921, the French government purchased one of his works, and in 1925, he was made a member of the Legion of Honor. By the 1930s, his reputation as one of the great figures of modern art was clear, and he was the subject of numerous books, articles, and exhibits. Between 1930 and 1931, his work went on show in Basel, Berlin, New York, and Paris.

Since he had begun spending his winters in Nice, on the French Riviera, Matisse had rarely done any traveling other than the journey from Paris to the south of France. During the 1930s, however, he began to travel extensively again. In 1930, he went to America. While he was there, he traveled to Merion, Pennsylvania, to meet Dr. Albert C. Barnes, the main American collector of his work.

Barnes commissioned Matisse to paint a large mural for the Barnes Foundation building in Merion, which housed the doctor's art collection.

The Snail, 1953, by Henri Matisse

This is one of Matisse's most famous "paper cutouts." The artist was drawing in bed one day when he came up with the idea of using pieces of colored paper to represent the circular shell of a snail. "The paper cutout," he said "allows me to draw in color.... Instead of drawing the outline and putting the color inside it ... I draw straight into the color."

Matisse carried out the project in Nice during 1931 and 1932, working in an old film studio since his normal studio was not big enough. But when the artist delivered the finished mural, it was clear that he had been given the wrong measurements: the work did not fit the intended space. Matisse started again and painted *The Dance II*, which is now displayed at the Barnes Foundation.

Now rich and famous, Matisse continued to work passionately. Besides paintings, he produced a range of other work, including sculpture, book illustrations, and designs for theaters.

By this time, World War II was about to break out. Matisse considered emigrating, but decided to stay in France. He made the south of the country his permanent home, living in a hotel suite in Nice. He was looked after by Lydia Delektorskaya, a Russian woman who

---

"I think only of rendering my sensations...." (Matisse on his aim in painting)

---

had modeled for him in the 1930s and who now became his housekeeper, secretary, and friend.

In 1941, Matisse had two operations for duodenal cancer. Surprised and grateful to survive them, the artist felt he had been granted another life, and continued working at an extraordinary rate. He even worked from his bed, fixing charcoal onto long poles and drawing on the walls and ceiling.

As the war progressed, Nice became a potential target for Italian invasion. In 1943, therefore, Matisse moved to the more secluded hill town of Vence. Here Matisse was persuaded to undertake the most important project of his last years. After his operations, he had

been nursed by one of his ex-models, now a nun in a Vence convent. In 1948, she persuaded him to design a chapel for the nuns —the Chapel of the Rosary, a work he completed in 1951. Matisse said the chapel expressed "the nearly religious feeling I have for life."

CREATIVE LAST YEARS

Matisse was too frail to attend the consecration of the chapel, but he still continued to work with enthusiasm. Increasingly confined to a wheelchair or to bed, he produced "paper cutouts." In a method similar to collage, he cut out shapes of brightly colored paper and pasted them on a background sheet, in order to create large and exuberant abstract works.

Matisse did the cutting himself, and then his assistants placed the pieces where he wanted them. The colors were so dazzling that Matisse's doctor advised him to wear dark glasses while he worked. He died peacefully at Nice on November 3, 1954, at the age of 84.

MAJOR WORKS	
1904	LUXE, CALME ET VOLUPTÉ
1905	WOMAN WITH A HAT; OPEN WINDOW, COLLIOURE; MADAME MATISSE
1932-33	THE DANCE
1952	LA TRISTESSE DU ROI (SORROW OF THE KING)
1953	THE SNAIL

PIET MONDRIAN

A shy, quiet man, Mondrian was dedicated to his work. With his distinctive patterns of black lines and colored squares, the Dutch painter became one of the most influential figures in the development of abstract art.

Piet Mondrian was born on March 7, 1872, in the quiet Dutch town of Amersfoort. His father, the headmaster of a local school and a traveling preacher, was frequently away from home. His mother was often sick, so most of the time Piet and his elder sister, Johanna, looked after the rest of the family.

Mondrian was a quiet boy, and found it difficult to make friends. Emotional stress often brought on bouts of illness and a sense of despair. Drawing and painting were his only comforts.

In 1892, he enrolled in the Amsterdam Art Academy. He did not join in student life in bustling Amsterdam, but lodged with friends of his father's, a wealthy and religious family.

In 1897, at the end of his studies, Mondrian went to live in the countryside. There, he spent a number of years quietly painting scenes of rural life and landscapes. But gradually, he became more interested in emphasizing the artificial nature of painting than in trying to create an illusion of the world.

In 1908, Mondrian made a breakthrough. He had seen work by a Dutch member of the avant-garde group, the Fauves. These artists painted in vivid, nonnaturalistic colors. Following their example, Mondrian applied bright, pure colors straight from the tube.

Within a year, Mondrian had become a leading member of the modern art movement in Holland. His work was exhibited and sold in the Netherlands. That same year, however, two events suddenly subdued his explosion of color. His mother died unexpectedly, and he broke off his engagement to a young Dutch woman, Greet Heybroek.

MOVING TO ABSTRACTION

Mondrian now adopted a flatter, colder style, and his work began to include secret, symbolic meanings. This reflected his new interest in theosophy, a

Self-portrait, 1918, by Piet Mondrian
In this portrait, the quiet and reserved painter shows himself standing in front of one of his early abstract works.

Composition in Red, Gray, Blue, Yellow, and Black, 1924-25, by Piet Mondrian
From 1919, Mondrian painted many diamond-shaped pictures. For him, the diagonal edges
of the canvas created a balance with the vertical and horizontal thrusts of the black lines.

religion based on the belief that true knowledge comes only from God, not through the senses or rational thought.

In 1911, Mondrian left the Netherlands for Paris. He discovered the paintings of Pablo Picasso (*see page 26*) and Georges Braque, the leaders of Cubism, a style of art in which objects are broken down into their elements. Their work greatly influenced him, and over the next three years, he worked on a series of Cubist paintings on the theme of a tree. In each picture, the image became more and more abstract, as Mondrian broke down the tree's form into black lines and patches of color.

When World War I broke out in 1914, Mondrian returned to Amsterdam. By this time, his paintings had lost all reference to identifiable objects. They were made up of little more than colored squares cut by little dashes of black line.

Mondrian's art excited many of the leading Dutch modern artists. He began to work with the painter Theo van Doesburg, launching a magazine, *De Stijl—The Style*—in 1917. In this, he put forward theories and ideas that would have a huge influence not only on art, but also on architecture and design.

On returning to Paris in 1919, Mondrian discovered that his own advances in painting had not been matched in his favorite city. He felt isolated, and despaired about his next move. He even told van Doesburg that he was giving up art to work in a vineyard in the south of France. He remained in Paris, however, and continued to paint.

FURTHER ABSTRACTION

Mondrian's work now became more abstract. He arranged his canvases on a grid of black lines, filling in squares with black, gray, white, and primary colors. This style—which he called "neoplasticism"—reflected his belief in theosophy, which claimed that humankind must rid itself of all objects before being able to reach truth. Through abstraction, he believed, he could express "the serene emotion of the universal."

The artist's output slowed down. His method required careful planning and constant repainting; a picture might take months to complete. For Mondrian, the position of the black lines and the white areas was all-important. The nature of his work demanded a withdrawal from society. His life was now as free of detail as his paintings.

During the 1920s and 1930s, Mondrian perfected his style. His works contained less color, and the white spaces and black lines dominated the canvas. He squeezed the colored areas to the painting's edge or removed them. In these works, he at last achieved his life's aim—a sense of peace.

In 1940, he moved to New York to escape World War II. Mondrian loved the city, and was truly happy for perhaps the first time in his life. In America, his work took on the rhythms of jazz, which he loved to listen to while painting. In his *Broadway Boogie Woogie*, for example, he replaced the black lines with rhythmic lines of broken color bordering white spaces. Mondrian was working on the follow-up, *Victory Boogie Woogie*, when he came down with pneumonia. He died on February 1, 1944, at the age of 77.

MAJOR WORKS

1912	THE FLOWERING APPLE TREE
1917	COMPOSITION
1924-25	COMPOSITION IN RED, GRAY, BLUE, YELLOW, AND BLACK
1942-43	BROADWAY BOOGIE WOOGIE

PAUL KLEE

Klee's work is among the most varied and complex of any 20th-century artist. Inspired as much by his imagination as by his experiences and travels, he used bright and radiant colors to express moods, emotions, and sensations.

Paul Klee was born on December 18, 1879, at Münchenbuchsee, near Berne in Switzerland. As a child, Paul was an accomplished violinist, and showed ability as a poet, but his main interest lay in painting. In 1898, at the age of 19, he moved to Munich, the most important artistic center in the region. He took lessons at a private art school, before studying at Munich Art Academy.

After a year-long tour of Italy, Klee returned home to Berne in 1902. He spent the next few years producing prints and drawings. There were few buyers for his work, however, so he earned extra money by playing in Berne's orchestra. In 1906, he married a pianist, Lily Stumpf, and moved back to Munich. There, Klee could keep in touch with the latest artistic trends.

THE BLUE RIDER

By 1911, he was in contact with one of the city's avant-garde art groups, *Der Blaue Reiter*—The Blue Rider. This circle, which included Franz Marc and Wassily Kandinsky (*see page 8*), believed that color could arouse powerful feelings. Klee was interested in their theory that colors could be "played" like music, with two working together in harmony, or with several forming visual chords to evoke certain moods.

The full impact of color on Klee's work became apparent after his trip to Tunisia, North Africa, in 1914. The shock of the intense sunlight and exotic sights was an overwhelming experience for Klee. Inspired, he began a series of brightly colored watercolors and oil paintings. He was so busy that he seemed untouched by the outbreak of World War I in August 1914. But when two of his closest friends from the *Blaue Reiter* group were later killed in battle, he fell into a deep depression.

In 1916, Klee himself was drafted into the German army. Since he was too

Man in Chair, 1913, by Gabriele Münter **Münter, Kandinsky's mistress, painted this portrait of Klee shortly after he became involved with the *Blaue Reiter* group.**

The Golden Fish, 1925, Paul Klee
Klee was always fascinated by aquariums, and marine life often featured in his work. Here, the artist has used simple, childlike shapes to create a dark, mysterious vision of the sea. The dazzling golden fish forms a striking contrast with the other underwater creatures.

old for active duty—he was now 37—he spent most of the war as a clerk at a training school for pilots. This enabled him to continue his painting.

When the war was over, Klee finally began to receive the recognition he had been seeking. By 1920, three books had been written about his work, and critics had warmly received an exhibit of his work in Munich. He was also offered a job at the Bauhaus, the revolutionary art school in Weimar, Germany. The post brought Klee financial security, and the opportunity to work closely with fellow artists. He particularly enjoyed the company of his old friend Kandinsky.

In 1925, a public gallery in Germany bought one of Klee's works. In the same year, he took part in the first exhibit of Surrealist art in Paris. One of the Surrealist poets, André Breton, hailed Klee as an ally of their movement. This was not strictly true: While Surrealist artists tried to represent the mysteries of the unconscious mind, Klee believed that the real world was "the essential point of departure for all artistic creation."

KLEE'S INSPIRATION
Many of the recognizable objects in Klee's paintings, therefore, originated from things he saw in his everyday life.

The twittering birds and glowing fish he painted stem from his visits to zoos and aquariums; other forms can be traced to the pebbles, fossils, and pressed leaves that he stored in his studio. The curious hieroglyphics, and the hints of desert landscapes and ruined cities, reflected his frequent travels abroad.

The place that had the greatest influence was Egypt, which he visited in the winter of 1928 and 1929. The visit lasted only three weeks, but the experience was decisive. The effect of the light, the open desert, and the ruined monuments created a powerful impression on Klee.

Increasingly, though, the artist's career was overshadowed by events closer to home. A change of management at the Bauhaus made him unhappy, and in 1931, he accepted a new post at the Düsseldorf Academy. This seemed ideal, since it gave him more time to concentrate on his painting. But his happy situation did not last long.

FORCED INTO EXILE

In 1933, Hitler's Nazis came to power in Germany. They were determined to suppress all forms of modern art, which they thought was dangerous. Artists and teachers like Klee were fired, and later their work was held up to ridicule in an exhibit entitled "Degenerate Art." Seventeen of Klee's paintings went on show alongside those by other members of the German avant-garde. In the face of such hostility, Klee left Germany and returned to Berne.

His later years were productive, and he enjoyed new fame in his native country after a major exhibit in 1935.

But his happiness at this success was clouded by illness. Initially diagnosed as bronchitis, it was later found to be a rare disease called scleroderma, which slowly attacks the whole body. Klee was still able to work, but now the mood of his pictures was somber. In place of his usual playfulness and humor, the images were stark and tragic.

"Color possesses me .... Color and I are one. I am a painter." (Paul Klee)

Occasional visitors made these last years more bearable. In 1937, famous artists like Pablo Picasso (*see page 26*) and Georges Braque came to see the artist, giving him a valuable sense of being in contact with the outside world.

Klee's condition worsened as World War II began. In May 1940, he entered a nursing home. He died on June 29, at the age of 60.

MAJOR WORKS

1914	MOTIF OF HAMMAMET
1922	THE TWITTERING MACHINE; SENECIO
1925	FISH MAGIC; GOLDEN FISH
1932	AD PARNASSUM
1940	DEATH AND FIRE

PABLO PICASSO

The most famous and original artist of the 20th century, Picasso is a legendary figure. His controversial paintings and sculptures—often inspired by his turbulent love life—dominated modern art before World War II.

Pablo Ruiz Picasso was born on March 25, 1881, in Málaga, then a quiet port in southern Spain famous for its bullfighting. He was the only boy in the family, and with his good looks and playful nature, his many relatives in Málaga spoiled him.

AN ARTISTIC CHILD

As a child, Picasso never wanted to do anything but paint. He refused to go to school unless he could keep some paintbrushes with him. His father, José —a struggling artist, who also taught art and ran the local museum—recognized his son's talent at an early age, and encouraged his ambitions. He gave Picasso his first art lessons.

In 1895, the family moved to Barcelona, northeast Spain, where Picasso's father had taken a teaching job at an art academy. Picasso enrolled at the academy and was put into the advanced class. But he soon became bored with the traditional teaching methods at the school. Instead, he took his inspiration from Barcelona's lively artistic scene. He often visited the city's cafés, spending hours listening to painters discussing the latest developments in art.

Barcelona was just a stepping stone, however. Picasso had his sights set on the cultural center of Europe: Paris. He finally arrived in the French capital in 1900, settling in Montmartre, on the edge of the city. He spent his days studying the works of art in the Louvre Museum. He also sought out the work of the leading artists of the day, such as Paul Cézanne and Henri de Toulouse-Lautrec.

During his first years in Paris, Picasso shared a room with the poet and journalist, Max Jacob. Neither of them had much money. They were so poor that Picasso had to burn bundles of his drawings to keep warm. His work at that time reflects this hardship. The artist painted sad and lonely subjects,

Pablo Picasso, 1953, by René Henry
Toward the end of his career, Picasso lived like a star. Here, he appears at the opening night of the 1953 Cannes film festival.

such as street musicians and beggars, to represent poverty and despair. His haunting, thin figures appeared against empty backgrounds of cold blues. This period of Picasso's art is now known as his "Blue Period."

LOVE AND CREATIVITY

In 1905, Picasso met the first love of his life, Fernande Olivier. Their relationship, which lasted until 1912, helped to lift the artist's gloom, and led to a burst of creative energy. The melancholy of his "Blue Period" now made way for the graceful serenity and warm sensuality of his "Rose Period." His subjects became livelier and more positive than they had been before: acrobats, dancers, and harlequins. Picasso worked hard at night, going to bed at dawn and getting up for breakfast at four in the afternoon. There were rumors that he was producing three canvases a day. His hard work was worth it: The "Rose" paintings sold well, and soon the artist's days of poverty were over for good.

Picasso now became the center of a circle of avant-garde artists, which included Henri Matisse (*see page 12*). Although Picasso respected Matisse as a painter, he had little interest in the Frenchman's abstract use of color. Picasso was more concerned with finding new ways to represent objects and figures than simply creating effects with color. He described his and Matisse's styles as "North and South poles."

In 1907, Picasso produced his most revolutionary painting—*Les Demoiselles d'Avignon*. With this work, which shows a group of women, the painter

THE CUBIST REVOLUTION

Picasso and Braque's startling innovations marked a turning point in modern art.

In 1908, Picasso began to work with his friend, Georges Braque. Although both artists wanted to represent the real world, they rejected the idea that art must be an exact imitation of nature. Slowly, they developed Cubism.

Picasso's *Violin and Guitar* (*right*) is typical of their first Cubist phase. He and Braque broke down objects into sets of cubes and rectangles, and then rebuilt them in overlapping patterns, scattering recognizable parts—a fragment of lettering, a bottle, a violin—throughout the picture. Often, they also showed the objects from different viewpoints at the same time.

moved away from trying to create an illusion of the real world. He twisted and distorted the faces and bodies of the figures, and placed them in a strange, unreal space. He even painted one of the women from several viewpoints, showing her front, back, and sides at once. This was a groundbreaking innovation that overthrew the traditional conventions of Western art.

In 1912, Braque and Picasso, added a new method. They now took ready-made fragments, such as bits of wallpaper, newspaper, and cloth, and built them up into collages of solid images.

Although their pictures are often difficult to decipher, Picasso and Braque always depicted real objects. But by breaking with the traditional methods of representation, they led the way toward a purely abstract art.

At the same time, Picasso rejected traditional ideas of beauty, giving some of the women startling masklike faces that show the influence of African art.

A FRUITFUL PARTNERSHIP

The astonishing work overwhelmed everyone who saw it, even Picasso's friends. These included the painter Georges Braque. Shortly after, he and Picasso began to work together, setting out to challenge the conventions of art yet further. They worked constantly, in Paris during the winter, and in the country during the summer. The result of their collaboration was Cubism, which by 1910 had become the leading avant-garde movement in French art.

The outbreak of World War I in 1914 halted the partnership, however. Braque enlisted, but Picasso, as a Spaniard, was exempt. Other friends also joined up, and Picasso felt lonely and isolated, making it difficult for him to work.

But two years later, the writer and artist Jean Cocteau took Picasso to

> "Painting is stronger than I am. It makes me do what it wishes."
> (Pablo Picasso)

Rome to design the scenery and costumes for a ballet, *Parade*. In Italy, Picasso studied the art of the Renaissance masters, Michelangelo and Raphael. He also fell in love with Olga Koklova, a dancer in the ballet. Olga and Picasso married in Paris in July 1918.

Picasso now became famous in Paris high society, attending all the most fashionable parties. He moved to a desirable area of the city, and gradually lost touch with his old friends.

He continued to produce Cubist still lifes and landscapes. But when Olga

Les Demoiselles d'Avignon, 1907, by Pablo Picasso
A landmark in modern art, this painting shocked Picasso's contemporaries. Its strange sense of space and terrifying, deformed figures still haunt and unsettle to this day.

became pregnant in 1920, he began a series of mother and child paintings. Their son, Paulo, was born in 1921.

Throughout the 1920s and 1930s, Picasso frequently changed his style. He was aware of new developments in art, but nothing distracted him from his search for new means of expressing the human form. Picasso continued to distort his female figures, culminating in *The Three Dancers* of 1925. This was perhaps a reflection of his own dissatisfaction with Olga. In 1927, Picasso began an affair with Marie-Thérèse Walter. When she became pregnant in 1935, Picasso asked Olga for a divorce. Even after their marriage ended, Olga remained in the background of his life until her death in 1955. She wrote him abusive letters, and would turn up at exhibits to scream insults at him.

No sooner had Marie-Thérèse given birth to a girl, Maia, than Picasso found a new love in Dora Maar, a photographer. Dora was temperamental, and their relationship was stormy.

GUERNICA

In 1936, Picasso was in Spain when General Franco led a military uprising against the Republican government. Soon, the country descended into a bloody civil war that would last two years and result in victory for Franco's rebels. At the start of the fighting, Picasso threw himself into the defense of the republic. He offered his support by accepting the directorate of the Prado state art museum in Madrid.

In 1937, he began work on a government commission to produce a mural for the International Exhibit in Paris. Picasso depicted the destruction of a little Spanish town, Guernica, which the Nazis had bombed on behalf of Franco. He finished the vast canvas in just a month. Painted in blacks and grays, the work expresses the horror of war.

When World War II broke out in 1939, Picasso was back in Paris, where he stayed until the end of the war. In 1943, Picasso met and fell in love with a 21-year-old model, Françoise Gilot. Their affair made Dora's disturbed mental state worse, prompting a breakdown.

In 1946, Picasso—now famous throughout the world, and commanding enormous prices for his work—moved with Françoise to the south of France. But Françoise hated the lack of privacy there: Picasso was treated like a star wherever he went. The birth of two children, Claude and Paloma, failed to keep their relationship alive, and in 1953, Françoise left. Jacqueline Roque quickly took her place.

Although Picasso continued to work at an astonishing rate, producing thousands of drawings, paintings, and sculptures, he needed the stimulus of other artists. But after 1945, the center of modern art had moved to New York, while Picasso remained in Europe. Cut off in this way, he slowly retreated from the art world. He bought a château in Provence, southern France, and became a virtual hermit. Even so, his late work is now recognized as a remarkable period of creativity. Eventually, two operations and failing eyesight halted his work. On April 8, 1973, he died, aged 91.

MAJOR WORKS

1903	THE OLD GUITARIST
1905	THE ACROBAT'S FAMILY
1907	LES DEMOISELLES D'AVIGNON
1913	VIOLIN AND GUITAR
1925	THE THREE DANCERS
1937	GUERNICA

DIEGO RIVERA

Inspired by his radical political beliefs, Rivera wanted to create an art for the masses. His monumental murals, glorifying the people and history of his native Mexico, were influential both in his own country and the United States.

José Diego Maria Rivera was born on December 13, 1886, in the silver-mining town of Guanajuato, Mexico. In 1892, his family moved to the capital, Mexico City. There, Diego showed a talent for drawing. In December 1896, he enrolled in evening classes at the Academy of San Carlos. He completed the full seven-year course at the academy, and then set his sights on Europe.

EUROPEAN INFLUENCES

In January 1907, Rivera left Mexico for Madrid. He did not remain long in Spain, however, and in 1909, he settled in Paris. Apart from a brief visit to Mexico in 1910, this was to be his home for the next 12 years. He soon became involved with the city's avant-garde artists. He was particularly interested in the work of the Cubists. In 1914, he met both Georges Braque and Pablo Picasso (*see page 26*), the founders of the movement. Picasso encouraged him until he decided that Rivera's style was growing too close to his own.

While in Paris, Rivera moved in with a Russian artist, Angeline Beloff. In 1912, he went with her to Spain to work for the summer. Three years later, Rivera left Angeline to live with another Russian artist, Marevna Vorobív-Stebelska, who was also experimenting with Cubism. Rivera asked Marevna to marry him, but she refused because Angeline was pregnant with the painter's baby. This child died in infancy. Soon after, Marevna bore Rivera a daughter.

By now, Rivera had abandoned Cubism, and was entering a decisive new phase of his career. In 1919, he traveled to Italy. He spent 17 months there, studying the frescoes of the Italian Renaissance. In these large wall paintings, or murals, he believed that he had discovered an art for the people. He thought that, just as the Renaissance artists had used murals in churches to

Diego Rivera, 1940, by Fritz Henle
Rivera may be considered unattractive, but he was irresistible to women. He was married three times and had numerous affairs.

The Formation of the Revolutionary Leadership (detail), 1926-27, by Diego Rivera
Rivera's mural cycle in the chapel at the National School of Agriculture, Chapingo, illustrated the school's slogan "Exploitation of the Land, not of Man," and dealt with the regeneration of Mexico after the Revolution. This panel shows a peasant standing up to a cruel landowner and his armed guards as they threaten other workers in the field.

communicate the lessons of Christianity to large congregations, so he too could use modern frescoes to convey political messages and ideas to the people of his own country.

THE MURALS

Rivera did not have to wait long to put this idea into practice. In the summer of 1921, he left behind his friends in Paris, and returned to Mexico. The country had just suffered a decade of political chaos and civil war following the Mexican Revolution of 1910. The turmoil had ended in 1920, when Álvaro Obregón took power, and began a massive program of regeneration and social reform. At the heart of the scheme was a major project for decorating public buildings with murals that captured the mood of the new beginning.

Rivera was one of the artists commissioned to work on the project, and in 1922, he began his first mural, *The Creation*, at the National Preparatory School. The following year, he was asked to paint the walls of the Ministry of Education. This was a mammoth task consisting of 117 panels covering 17,200 square feet. It took him more than four years to complete the job, partly because he was also working on murals for the National School of Agriculture at Chapingo at the same time. In order to meet the punishing schedule, Rivera often ate and slept on the scaffolding. This nearly resulted in disaster when, in 1927, he fell off while he was asleep and seriously injured himself.

By now, Rivera had become deeply involved in politics. He was an active member of the Mexican Communist party, and he was president of a radical labor organization. As a result, many of his murals were overtly political, containing Communist images, and glorifying the people, industry, and culture

---

> "Mexican mural painting made the masses the hero of a monumental art." (Diego Rivera)

---

of Mexico with a revolutionary fervor. These works helped Rivera become a national hero throughout Mexico.

A TURBULENT MARRIAGE

In August 1929, Rivera married a fellow artist, Frida Kahlo (*see page 36*). They made an unlikely looking couple: While Rivera was a huge man, Kahlo was tiny. Her parents likened it to "a marriage between an elephant and a dove." It was a stormy marriage, with affairs on both sides. At one point, they divorced, but soon remarried. Diego was heartbroken when Frida died in 1954.

Also in 1929, Rivera began work on the *History of Mexico* murals at the National Palace. This was his most ambitious scheme of all, showing events from a thousand years of the country's history, with an eagle—symbol of Mexico's pride and strength—at the center.

Word of his designs spread, and in 1930 he was invited to the United States to work on some major projects. He created murals for the San Francisco Stock Exchange, the California School of Arts, and the Detroit Institute of Arts. He also painted a mural for Rockefeller Center in New York City. The painting contained a portrait of the Russian Communist leader, Lenin. An outcry followed. When Rivera refused to remove the detail, Rockefeller fired him, and destroyed the mural.

STRAIN AND STRUGGLE

Rivera returned to Mexico in low spirits. A drastic diet had left him weak, and his relationship with Kahlo was increasingly strained. His political beliefs were also hampering his career in Mexico: Socialism was now thought undesirable by the government, which was seeking the support of the United States. Between 1935 and 1943, he received no government commissions.

Instead, Rivera now concentrated his energies on building a massive, temple-like home, *Anahuacalli*. He died of a heart attack at his studio on November 24, 1957, at the age of 70, and was buried with official honors.

MAJOR WORKS

1922	THE CREATION
1923-28	MINISTRY OF EDUCATION CYCLE
1926-27	CHAPINGO CHAPEL CYCLE
1929-30	HISTORY OF MEXICO CYCLE
1932-33	DETROIT INDUSTRY

FRIDA KAHLO

Despite enduring great pain throughout her life, Kahlo achieved artistic recognition both in her native Mexico and abroad. Her intensely personal paintings reflect her physical torment and her marriage to the artist, Diego Rivera.

Frida Kahlo was born on July 6, 1907, in Coyoacán, a suburb of Mexico City. At the age of six, she had polio. Her right leg grew thinner, and her foot became deformed, earning her the cruel nickname "Peg-Leg Frida."

Further physical suffering was to come. On September 17, 1925, the school bus she was on crashed, killing several people. Kahlo survived, but a metal handrail penetrated her body. Her right leg and pelvic bone were broken, her spine fractured, and her right foot crushed: She would be in pain for the rest of her life. After the accident, Kahlo had to spend a year in a hospital. To defy the boredom of her recovery, she took up painting. Her first picture was a self-portrait, setting the pattern for her career. Most of her works would be portraits of either herself or her friends.

In around 1927, Kahlo met Diego Rivera (*see page 32*), Mexico's most famous artist. From the early 1920s, Rivera had been painting murals to teach the public about the government's reform aims. By the end of the decade, he was a national hero. He recognized Kahlo's talent and encouraged her.

A STORMY MARRIAGE

On August 21, 1929, Kahlo married Rivera, who was 21 years her elder. The couple's marriage was passionate but stormy. Rivera was a notorious womanizer, and Kahlo, too, had secret affairs. Yet their marriage provided a source of strength for both artists. Under Rivera's influence, Kahlo's style changed, and became much more clearly Mexican.

In 1930, Rivera and Kahlo moved to the United States, where Rivera had commissions to work on some prestigious projects. The couple stayed there for the next four years. Rivera was fascinated by their new home, but Kahlo was less happy. She expressed her feelings in *Self-portrait on the Borderline between Mexico and the*

Frida Kahlo, 1944
This photograph shows the artist when she was 37 years old.

Self-portrait, 1947, by Frida Kahlo
Kahlo's caption explains that this is her mirror image. It also gives her age as 37, even though she was 40 at the time. This is because the artist, a proud patriot, claimed to have been born in 1910, so that her birth coincided with the start of the Mexican Revolution.

United States. While the left half of the painting, filled with references to Mexico, is flooded with warm sunlight, the American half is cloudy and dark.

Kahlo's years in the United States were fruitful, however. She produced many works, and met fellow artists all over the country. In 1931, she exhibited in public for the first time, with the San Francisco Society of Women Artists. In the same year, she painted a portrait of the famous horticulturalist, Luther Burbank, who had died five years earlier. Kahlo depicted him as half-man and half-tree. By doing this, she was moving away from straightforward representation, and applying, for the first time, her highly unique use of symbols.

This period of Kahlo's life was overshadowed by two miscarriages. That she could not bear children was perhaps the most distressing effect of her childhood accident. On their return to Mexico in 1934, Kahlo and Rivera moved into a newly built house, consisting of two cubes connected by a long bridge. The building was symbolic of a widening gap between the couple. By this time, Rivera had begun an affair with Kahlo's sister, Christina.

INTERNATIONAL SUCCESS

Despite these traumas, one of Kahlo's most successful working periods now began. In the spring of 1938, Kahlo met André Breton, a French poet who was closely involved with avant-garde painters in Paris. This gave her an opportunity to discover the recent developments in European art. In the same year, Kahlo exhibited her work in a prominent New York gallery. The exhibit was a success, and Kahlo sold 12 out of 25 paintings.

The next year, Breton organized an exhibit of Kahlo's work in Paris. But 1939 also brought anguish. Kahlo and Rivera separated, and in November finally divorced. But they soon discovered they could not live without one another. They remarried within a year.

Kahlo's success abroad was followed by recognition in her own country. In 1942, she became one of 25 members of a government organization set up to promote Mexican culture. The following year, she was invited to teach at the College of Sculpture, where pupils were encouraged to work in a Mexican style. Many of Kahlo's famous self-portraits date from this period.

A PAINFUL END

In the mid-1940s, Kahlo's health deteriorated dramatically. In 1950, she had to spend nine months in the hospital. She was still able to paint while lying in bed, but only for five hours a day. Her paintings were now mostly still lifes: looking into the mirror had become too painful. After 1951, she took painkillers constantly. Against medical advice, in 1953 she attended the opening of her first solo exhibit in Mexico City.

In August that year, the doctors amputated Kahlo's right leg, and she lost her will to live. She died on July 12, 1954. The official diagnosis was "pulmonary embolism," or a blockage of a blood vessel. The last entry in her diary, however, suggests joy and relief, leading some experts to speculate that she committed suicide.

MAJOR WORKS

1926	SELF-PORTRAIT WEARING A VELVET DRESS
1931	FRIDA AND DIEGO RIVERA; PORTRAIT OF LUTHER BURBANK
1932	THE FLYING BED
1944	THE BROKEN COLUMN
1946	THE WOUNDED DEER

ROBERT FROST

During his long lifetime, Robert Frost captivated millions with his classic, plain-speaking poetry. His expressive, passionate descriptions of the natural world made him the true heir of the Romantic poets.

Robert Lee Frost was born in California on March 26, 1874. He spent his early years in San Francisco with his father, William Prescott Frost, who was a journalist and politician, his Scottish mother, Isabelle, and his sister, Jeanie.

Life for the Frosts was not easy. Jeanie Frost, two years younger than Robert, was mentally unstable. She would spend the last decade of her life in a hospital for the insane. There was a tendency in the family toward mental illness, and this would worry Robert throughout his life.

MEETING ELINOR

In 1885, William Frost died of tuberculosis. Soon after, Isabelle traveled to Lawrence, Massachusetts, a cotton-mill town, and then to Salem, New Hampshire, where she taught school. Frost studied classics at Lawrence High School, graduating in 1892. There he became captivated by his co-valedictorian, Elinor White, and the two were married in a secret ceremony of their own creation. That fall, however, Elinor went to St. Lawrence University in New York State, where she had won a scholarship. Angry, Frost left for Dartmouth College, where he lasted just a few months before returning to Lawrence.

Robert and Elinor finally married in 1895. The quietly intelligent Elinor would always be a central figure in Frost's life. Life was hard: The couple shared an apartment with Robert's mother and sister, and helped teach in a small school Isabelle had opened. In 1896, their son, Elliott, was born.

In 1897, Frost entered Harvard, where he studied Greek, Latin, philosophy, and psychology. Frost's academic career was brilliant yet brief; he left after less than two years. He was under intense strain: Elinor was pregnant again, his mother was ill, and Frost was troubled by symptoms that he feared might mean he would die of tubercu-

Robert Frost, c.1926, by E.O. Hoppé
This somber photograph shows the writer in his early fifties.

losis, like his father. In 1899, Elinor had a daughter, Lesley, but her birth was followed by Elliott's death from cholera. In 1900, Frost's mother died of cancer.

A BOY'S WILL

Just before Isabelle Frost's death, Robert's grandfather bought him a farm in Derry, New Hampshire. The Frosts lived in Derry for ten peaceful years. It

---

> "I dropped to an everyday level of diction that even Wordsworth kept above."
> (Frost on *North of Boston*)

---

was here that Frost wrote the poems of his first collection, *A Boy's Will*.

In his poetry, Frost followed in the tradition of the Romantic poets, such as William Wordsworth. He wrote expressively about nature, particularly the "country things" of New England— woodpiles, orchards, birches, snowy woods, and pastures. The poems of *A Boy's Will* are romantic lyrics, with a general atmosphere of melancholy song, wind, rain, and ghosts.

In 1912, Frost took his family to England, where they rented a country cottage. The move was a good one. A British publisher accepted *A Boy's Will*, producing it in 1913. Frost then

THE SOUND OF SENSE

Frost discussed his poetic aims in letters and lectures. He wanted to create a natural, expressive voice.

One of Frost's main concerns in his poems was what he called "the sound of sense," or the importance of using ordinary speech in poetry.

Frost believed that a poet had to do more than merely choose certain words in order to convey a poem's meaning. He felt that he had to achieve the sound of what he called "running speech."

To do this, he created the natural rhythm of a "speaking tone" by using long, rambling sentences punctuated by conjunctions, as in everyday speech. The poem "After Apple-Picking," for example, begins with the conversational voice of a speaker

quickly completed the poems for a second volume, *North of Boston*, which was published the following year.

North of Boston is a short collection of dramatic monologues, together with a few odes such as the famous "After Apple-Picking." The poems in this second collection are very different from the first. By now, Frost had developed his theory that poetry should be written

who could be easily chatting casually to a neighbor about the apple harvest.

Frost's contribution to American poetry was recognized far beyond the confines of the literary world. In 1950, the U.S. Senate honored him on his 75th birthday. In 1961, President Kennedy invited the 86-year-old poet to read one of his poems at his inauguration (*above*).

in "the sound of speech." The style of the poems is therefore much plainer than in *A Boy's Will*. The characters in the poems range from farmhands and housewives to witches.

Frost maintained his own poetic style in the face of new, modernist poetry. Contemporary poets, such as T.S. Eliot, were breaking down the traditional way of writing, and attempting to ex-

press the fragmented nature of the 20th century in their work. To many, Frost's poetry was outdated: It did not deal with the modern world. Yet to millions of others, Frost was the ultimate poet of nature—the true heir of Wordsworth.

By the time *North of Boston* was published, Frost was famous. For the rest of his long life, he made a living as a traveling poet. He lectured, read, or taught at a great many colleges in the United States. He also made a living from selling his original manuscripts.

A TRAGIC FAMILY

Frost's children had tragic lives. His daughter Marjorie died after the birth of her daughter; his son Carol shot himself, and his daughter Irma spent her life in an institution.

In 1938, Elinor died. Frost wrote his last great poem, "Directive," eight years later. Its inspiration was his return to Derry to scatter Elinor's ashes. "Directive" is about a journey backward in time, and expresses feelings of loss.

In his late years, Frost was respected all over the world. His poetry volumes included *In the Clearing* (1962). Robert Frost died in 1963, at the age of 88.

MAJOR WORKS

1913	A BOY'S WILL
1914	NORTH OF BOSTON
1942	A WITNESS TREE
1946	"DIRECTIVE"
1962	IN THE CLEARING

CARL SANDBURG

A true man of the people, Carl Sandburg was blessed with many talents. In addition to writing poetry that captured the spirit of his native Midwest, Sandburg was a celebrated musician, biographer, and historian.

Carl Sandburg was born on January 6, 1878, in Galesburg, Illinois, the first son of a Swedish immigrant family. His father, August, worked on the railroad. The family was very poor, and Carl had to leave school at 13 to find work. Over the next four years, he worked as a farm laborer, a milkman, and a bricklayer—to list just a few of his many jobs. At 17, he set off to live the life of a hobo. He worked his way through Kansas, Nebraska, and Colorado before finally returning to Galesburg, where he became a house painter's apprentice.

In 1898, the United States, outraged by the sinking of a battleship in Havana harbor, went to war with Spain, which ruled Cuba at the time. Sandburg enlisted in the army, and was stationed in Puerto Rico for eight months, although he never saw any fighting. One of Sandburg's friends in the army was a student at Lombard College, Galesburg. He persuaded Sandburg to enroll there himself on his return from military service.

Sandburg paid for his education by working part-time. It was at Lombard that he started writing. One of his professors encouraged him in this, and even published three books of Sandburg's poetry at his own expense. Despite this vote of confidence, Sandburg decided not to take his final exams, and in 1902, he set off once again on his travels around America. Eventually, he settled down in Milwaukee, where he found a job writing for a local newspaper. It was then that he met Lilian Steichen, whom he married in 1908. They would have three daughters.

CHICAGO

In 1912, Sandburg moved to Chicago. The energy and vitality of this rapidly industrializing city fired his imagination. It was here that Sandburg first achieved widespread recognition with "Chicago,"

Carl Sandburg
This undated photograph shows the poet with a copy of his study of American folk music, *The American Songbag*.

a poem that appeared in *Poetry: A Magazine of Verse*. This celebration of the "Stormy, husky, brawling" city, "Hog Butcher for the World," made him the leader of a group of exciting young writers based in Chicago, and in 1916, *Chicago Poems* was published to great acclaim. A succession of poetry collections followed, establishing Sandburg as one of America's most important poets.

A POET OF THE PEOPLE

Sandburg greatly admired the poetry of Walt Whitman. Like this poet, Sandburg wrote in free verse—a type of poetry which neither rhymes nor uses fixed rhythmic patterns. Sandburg drew on the ever-changing rhythms of ordinary speech, and he became known as "the poet of the Midwest" for his rendering of the vibrant dialect of his native region. In *Chicago Poems* he showed how expressive this language could be, with poems ranging from the angry city-slang of "To a Contemporary Bunkshooter" to the delicate imagery of "Fog."

During World War I, Sandburg worked as a foreign correspondent in Stockholm, Sweden. On his return to the States, he bought a home 60 miles east of Chicago, on the shores of Lake Michigan. Here he set to work on a biography of the 16th president of the United States, Abraham Lincoln. This work would occupy Sandburg for the next 20 years.

For a few months of each year, the writer would rest from this huge task and set off around the country to earn his living. He traveled with his guitar or banjo, singing folk songs and reciting

ABRAHAM LINCOLN

Sandburg celebrated the life of his hero, Abraham Lincoln, in one of the finest biographies ever written.

Published in 1926, *Abraham Lincoln: The Prairie Years*, was quickly recognized as a work of genius. By the time the second part, *Abraham Lincoln: The War Years*, was published, Sandburg was regarded as the world's foremost authority on America's 16th president (*right*). He enriched his research with poetic insight to produce a uniquely sensitive portrait. One reviewer described Sandburg's biography as "a monument that will stand forever—a monument to both subject and author alike."

From his childhood, Sandburg had been fascinated by Lincoln. Like the writer himself, the pres-

his own poems to crowded halls. The interpretation that his deep, powerful voice lent to his work was unforgettable, and he was much in demand. He was also an excellent guitarist, and sang traditional ballads in what one of his friends called "the voice of America singing." An expert on the folk music of America, he published *The American Songbag* in 1927.

the mass. Did you know that all the work of the world is done through me?"

The Depression of the 1930s was a time of great hardship for the poor in America. Sandburg was sharp in his criticism of the social injustice he saw around him, and thought it immoral that any country should tolerate such vast inequalities of wealth. Throughout his life, he was both a committed socialist and a great patriot, who believed firmly in the principles of equality and democracy enshrined in the Constitution.

LATER YEARS

Toward the end of his life, Sandburg was showered with honors. In 1953, he wrote *Always the Young Strangers*, a sensitive account of his childhood in Galesburg. He also continued to write fine poetry, publishing his last collection, *Honey and Salt*, in 1963. Sandburg died on July 22, 1967, at the age of 89. His last home, a farm in North Carolina, is a now a national historic site.

ident had been born into a poor family. Both of them had risen through talent and hard work. For Sandburg, Lincoln symbolized everything that was good about his country. Lincoln's example gave Sandburg a deep faith that America would realize its destiny to become a land in which justice and freedom were available to all.

Sandburg used his encyclopedic knowledge of folklore in his 1936 poem, *The People, Yes*, which he filled with folktales, proverbs, and legends. This poem shows Sandburg's deep concern for the American working classes, and his faith in their culture. He was proud of his own poor background, declaring in one of his most famous lines: "I am the people—the mob—the crowd—

MAJOR WORKS

1916	**CHICAGO POEMS**
1926	**ABRAHAM LINCOLN: THE PRAIRIE YEARS**
1927	**THE AMERICAN SONGBAG**
1936	**THE PEOPLE, YES**
1939	**ABRAHAM LINCOLN: THE WAR YEARS**
1953	**ALWAYS THE YOUNG STRANGERS**
1963	**HONEY AND SALT**

D.H. LAWRENCE

Lawrence scandalized his contemporaries with uncompromisingly honest and passionate novels such as *Lady Chatterley's Lover*. Yet he is now recognized as one of the greatest writers of his generation.

David Herbert Lawrence was born on September 11, 1885, in Eastwood, a coal-mining town in the north of England. His father, Arthur, was a miner who drank heavily, and his adoring mother, Lydia, was bright and lively. David was a delicate child, who preferred studying and nature to sport.

A BRIGHT BOY

Lydia was determined to keep her son out of the mines, so she encouraged his studies. When he was 13, David won a scholarship to the local high school. After three years, he got a job as a clerk, but a severe attack of pneumonia forced him to leave after three months.

While he was recovering, Lawrence started to visit his friend, Alan Chambers, who lived on a nearby farm. David became particularly close to Alan's sister, Jessie, with whom he went for long walks and spent hours reading literature. Their friendship would last nearly 12 years, despite the jealous disapproval of Lawrence's mother.

When Lawrence was fully recovered, he became a pupil-teacher at a school in Eastwood, teaching "savage collier lads" (young coal miners) while receiving instruction himself. In 1905, he gained one of the highest marks in England in the King's Scholarship Examination. The next year, he went to Nottingham University College, where he completed a two-year teaching course.

For the last six years, he had been writing poems. A few months after he began teaching in a suburb of London in 1908, Jessie sent some of these poems to the editor of the *English Review*. The magazine published them in 1909.

This success was marred by the death of Lawrence's mother from cancer in December 1910. Lawrence was too upset to enjoy the publication of his first novel, *The White Peacock*, the next month. Trying to overcome his grief, he became engaged to Louie Burrows. But

D.H. Lawrence, 1920, by Jan Juta
This dark and serious portrait shows the writer at the age of 35.

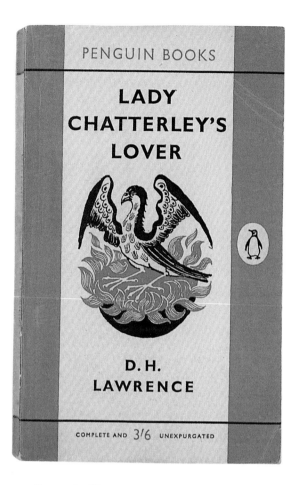

PENGUIN BOOKS

LADY CHATTERLEY'S LOVER

D. H. LAWRENCE

COMPLETE AND 3/6 UNEXPURGATED

Lady Chatterley's Lover, Penguin Unexpurgated Edition 1960
Penguin Books was the first publisher in England to risk producing a complete text of Lawrence's scandalous novel, in 1960—32 years after it was written. Penguin was prosecuted under the Obscene Publications Act, and acquitted after a celebrated trial.

he soon broke off the engagement, and returned to Eastwood.

In 1912, Lawrence visited his old professor, Ernest Weekley. He met Weekley's wife of 12 years, Frieda von Richthofen, the daughter of a German aristocrat. The lively, passionate Frieda was bored with her stuffy husband. Within just two months of meeting Lawrence, she had eloped with him.

A LIFELONG COMPANION

Lawrence adored Frieda, and although their relationship was stormy, he would stay with her for the rest of his life. She was strong-minded, and had a profound influence on Lawrence's work.

In 1912, Lawrence's second novel, *The Trespasser*, was published. It was not well-received, however. David and Frieda left England and traveled to Germany and Italy. Here he finished his third novel, *Sons and Lovers*.

Based on life at Eastwood, *Sons and Lovers* won critical acclaim when it appeared in 1913. Paul Morel, the son of a miner and a possessive mother, is drawn to Miriam Leivers, a shy farm girl. Morel rejects her love and seeks fulfillment with a married woman.

The conflict between Lawrence's mother and his friend Jessie provided him with valuable material. After reading the final version, however, Jessie was so hurt by the portrait of Miriam that she never spoke to the writer again.

DIFFICULT YEARS

Frieda and Lawrence were married in London in 1914—the year that World War I broke out. This would be a difficult period for the couple. The publication of *The Rainbow* in 1915 was part of their troubles. The novel, tracing three generations of the Brangwen family, contained controversial passages. The book was declared obscene and all copies were suppressed.

Disillusioned, the Lawrences moved to Cornwall. Here, the writer wrote *Women in Love*, continuing the story of one of the Brangwens, Ursula. He felt this was his finest novel. But it shocked the public, and was not published until 1920—and then only in America.

The Cornish locals suspected the Lawrences of being German spies, and they suffered persecution. Eventually, in October 1917, they were ordered to leave their cottage. Lawrence would never feel happy in England again.

In 1919, Lawrence traveled to Italy, and the following year, the couple settled in Sicily. The writer worked hard, producing travel books and poems, as well as fiction. He then traveled in Ceylon, Australia, and America, arriving in Taos, New Mexico in 1922.

Lawrence had been invited there by Mabel Dodge Sterne, a wealthy American. He fell in love with New Mexico, and moved with Frieda to a log cabin in the mountains outside Taos. In 1923, they moved to Chapala, Mexico, where Lawrence began writing *The Plumed Serpent*. But Frieda was restless, and persuaded him to return to England.

They came back to America in March 1924 and stayed at a ranch, Kiowa, that Sterne had given Frieda. Lawrence then traveled back to Mexico, where he finished his last novel. By now, he was very sick, and diagnosed as tubercular.

In September 1925, Lawrence left America. He spent most of the rest of his life in Italy. He continued to write poetry but completed only one more novel—*Lady Chatterley's Lover*. This is about a love affair between a rich mineowner's wife and a humble gamekeeper. Not Lawrence's finest work, it is his best known, mainly because of the scandal caused by the writer's explicit descriptions and his use of four-letter words. It was printed privately in Italy in 1928.

On February 6, 1930, Lawrence was admitted to a sanatorium in Vence, in the south of France. He left on March 1, and died the following day.

MAJOR WORKS

1911	THE WHITE PEACOCK
1913	SONS AND LOVERS
1915	THE RAINBOW
1920	WOMEN IN LOVE
1926	THE PLUMED SERPENT
1928	LADY CHATTERLEY'S LOVER

EUGENE O'NEILL

A restless, unhappy man, Eugene O'Neill spent a lifetime trying to understand his troubled childhood. Emotional, intense, and innovative, O'Neill's deeply autobiographical plays revolutionized American theater.

Eugene O'Neill was born in New York City on October 16, 1888. He was the youngest of three sons. Ella, his mother, was given morphine to ease the pain of Eugene's difficult birth—with tragic consequences. She became addicted to the drug, and would remain so for the next 26 years. Ella's addiction gave her a much-needed escape from reality. Her second son, Edmund, had recently died from measles, which he had caught from his brother, James.

TORTURED YOUTH

The two surviving boys were tortured with guilt: James for having given his younger brother measles, and Eugene for having been the cause of his mother's addiction. They had an unsettled childhood, living in a series of hotel rooms as they accompanied their father, an actor, on his tours. Both boys grew up confused and rebellious young men.

O'Neill's early life lacked any clear direction. In 1906, he entered Princeton, but left after a year to work for a New York mail order company. In 1909, he married a girl he knew, Kathleen Jenkins, but soon realized he had made a mistake. Although his new wife was pregnant, O'Neill left on a mining expedition to Central America. He then spent a year as a seaman. On his return to New York, he became depressed, and in January 1912, tried to commit suicide. That year, he divorced Kathleen.

O'Neill then joined his father's theater company for a few months, taking small acting roles. He spent the summer with his family in New London, Connecticut, and worked as a reporter on a local newspaper. But after six months, his health broke down. O'Neill spent the first half of 1913 in a sanatorium, recovering from tuberculosis, a disease of the lungs.

During his time in the sanatorium, O'Neill read widely, and decided to become a playwright. On recovering, he

Eugene O'Neill, 1938
This photograph shows the playwright at the age of 50, outside his home in Georgia.

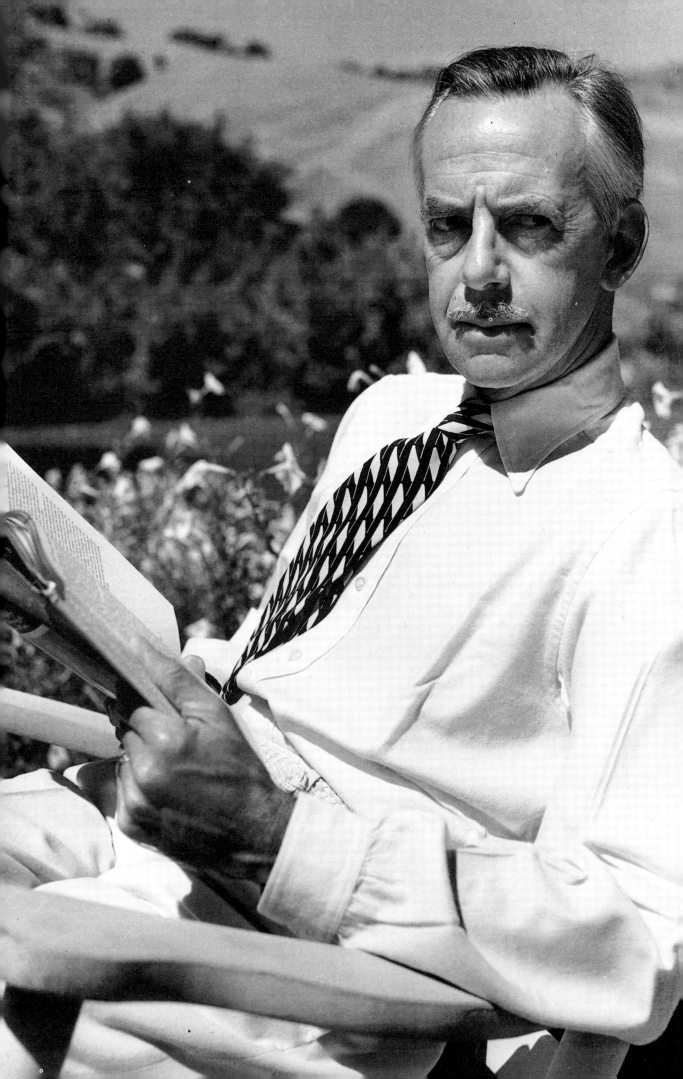

studied theater at Harvard for a year, and then returned to New York, where he mixed in artistic and literary circles. O'Neill's first theatrical opportunity came during a visit to an artists' colony in Provincetown, Massachusetts. The Provincetown Players, a small amateur theater company, produced O'Neill's *Bound East for Cardiff*, a one-act play which drew upon his experiences as a sailor. It premiered on July 28, 1916.

SUCCESS

In September 1916, the Provincetown Players moved to New York. In the next three years, they staged ten of O'Neill's plays. With their realistic settings and authentic dialogue, these plays differed from the action-packed, heroic melodramas that were popular at the time. In 1920, O'Neill's first full-length play, *Beyond the Horizon*, opened on Broadway, and received enthusiastic reviews. The next year, *Anna Christie* established O'Neill as America's most exciting and original playwright.

O'Neill's rise to prominence coincided with a time of personal change. In 1918, he had married the writer Agnes Boulton, with whom he had two children. Two years later, O'Neill's father died, followed in 1922 by his mother, and in 1923 by his brother. As the sole survivor of his family, O'Neill was now free to write about his troubled childhood—the subject of his finest plays. Ironically, however, he was blind to the suffering of his own children, whom he neglected terribly. In 1927, O'Neill left Agnes for an actress, Carlotta Monterey, whom he married two years later.

A FAMILY TRAGEDY

One of O'Neill's finest plays, *Long Day's Journey into Night* tells the tragic story of the writer's own family.

Long Day's Journey into Night is O'Neill's most autobiographical play. He stated that it should not be performed for 25 years after his death, so as not to offend any relatives. But the play was first performed just three years after O'Neill died, in 1956.

The story of James Tyrone, a miserly actor, his drug-addicted wife, and their tortured sons, is based entirely on that of the O'Neills. The play is set in 1912, the year in which O'Neill, like the play's younger son, developed tuberculosis. All the action takes place in an exact replica of his family's summer cottage in Connecticut (*above right*). The char-

The hallmark of O'Neill's work was a constant willingness to experiment. Whereas his early plays had been brutally realistic, by the mid 1920s, he had become influenced by expressionist drama—a type of play that sacrificed the illusion of reality in order to achieve striking emotional effects. In a play produced in 1926, *The Great God Brown*, for example, O'Neill masked all

acters in the play even share names with the real O'Neills.

O'Neill said that he wrote the play with "deep pity and understanding for *all* the four haunted Tyrones." Working on it was an emotional experience for him: His wife Carlotta said that O'Neill would come out of his study at the end of a day "gaunt and sometimes weeping."

his characters—a technique borrowed from the theater of the ancient Greeks, which he greatly admired.

O'Neill was not afraid of challenging his audience's expectations. *Strange Interlude*, a play produced in 1927, was so long that it had to be staged with an extended intermission, to give the audience a chance to eat dinner. His experiments were often criticized, but in

1936, he was rewarded with the Nobel Prize for Literature—the first time an American playwright had won the prize.

A TRAGIC VISION

Through all his many styles, one thing remained constant in O'Neill's work— a deep sense of the tragedy of life. *The Iceman Cometh*, written in 1939, for example, is about a group of characters who spend most of their time in a bar, dreaming of a brighter future. The "iceman," a traveling salesman, forces them to admit that their dreams are unfounded. The most pessimistic of O'Neill's plays, *Iceman* implies that happiness is a symptom of ignorance.

In his later years, O'Neill suffered from a hand tremor which by 1943 had forced him to give up writing. He died in Boston, of bronchial pneumonia, on November 27, 1953. He left several unseen plays, including one of his finest, the autobiographical *Long Day's Journey into Night*. When the play opened in New York on November 7, 1956— nearly 20 years after O'Neill had written it—the world hailed it as a masterpiece.

MAJOR WORKS

1913-14	BOUND EAST FOR CARDIFF
1918	BEYOND THE HORIZON
1920	ANNA CHRISTIE
1939	THE ICEMAN COMETH
1939-41	LONG DAY'S JOURNEY INTO NIGHT

F. SCOTT FITZGERALD

The spokesperson for the glittering "Jazz Age," Fitzgerald mirrored the glamour and excesses of his stories in his own life. A wild lifestyle, alcoholism, and a turbulent marriage shattered both his talent and his health.

Francis Scott Key Fitzgerald was born on September 24, 1896, in St. Paul, Minnesota. His father was a failed businessman who scraped a living selling groceries. The family had a generous inheritance on which they depended.

A FIERCE AMBITION

At St. Paul Academy, and later at boarding school, Scott became known as a show-off. He turned to writing as a way of gaining attention. In 1913, he went to Princeton University, where he began to write in earnest. Soon his talent began to earn him the celebrity he craved.

When he left Princeton, Fitzgerald had a clear ambition: "I want to be one of the greatest writers who ever lived." But the United States entry into World War I halted his plans. The 21-year-old joined the army in October 1917. While he was in training camp, he began writing a novel, which developed into *This Side of Paradise.*

In 1918, Fitzgerald fell in love with a lively and beautiful 18-year-old, Zelda Sayre. They seemed a perfect couple. Both were determined to achieve success—Zelda wanted to be a dancer—and fame. After leaving the army, Fitzgerald moved to New York and tried to establish himself as a writer.

He was not successful at first, but then, in 1919, a New York magazine editor accepted *This Side of Paradise.* Fitzgerald now began to sell his stories to the *Saturday Evening Post* magazine. Writing for magazines would prove his steadiest source of income.

Fitzgerald enjoyed his early success to the full, spending extravagantly. The future looked bright. In March 1920, *This Side of Paradise* was published to great critical acclaim, and the following month, Scott and Zelda were married.

At just 23, Fitzgerald was rich and famous. He rode on taxicab roofs and jumped into fountains, gave endless interviews, and drank champagne at

F. Scott Fitzgerald
This photograph shows the writer during the 1930s—the period of his downfall.

countless parties. "I had everything I wanted and knew I would never be so happy again," he wrote. But there was a darker side. He was drinking heavily, and he and Zelda were always fighting.

In October 1921, back home in St. Paul, the Fitzgerald's daughter, Scottie, was born. By now Scott had begun his second novel, *The Beautiful and the*

> ### "All the stories ... had a touch of disaster in them ... My million-aires were ... beautiful and damned"
> ### (F. Scott Fitzgerald)

Damned, published in 1922. His novels captured the frivolous lifestyles of couples like himself and Zelda. These couples waste and ruin their lives—and ultimately destroy each other.

GLAMOUR AND EXCESS

In 1922, the Fitzgeralds rented a house on Long Island. Here, they continued their extravagant lifestyle, frittering away thousands of dollars. After a spell on the French Riviera, they moved to Paris in 1925. Fitzgerald's third novel, *The Great Gatsby*, was published in 1925 to good reviews but poor sales.

By now, the Fitzgeralds' lifestyle had disintegrated into a nightmare of drama and excess. For some years, their marriage had been falling apart. Scott's drinking was getting worse. He shocked

THE GREAT GATSBY

Fitzgerald's timeless love story is also a fascinating social document of the glamorous "Jazz Age."

Fitzgerald's classic novel, *The Great Gatsby*, brings to life the 1920s—a period of prosperity and optimism in the United States known as the "Jazz Age." The narrator, Nick Carraway, observes the tragedy of the mysterious millionaire Jay Gatsby (*right*). Gatsby's dream is to win back his first love, Daisy, who is now married. Gatsby is obsessed with creating vast wealth and success in order to captivate Daisy, and throws glittering parties. Yet as he follows his dream, his ideals shatter around him.

The novel is dazzling in its portrayal of a constant whirlwind of parties, glamour, beauty, and ex-

guests with his wild behavior: At one dinner party, he attacked a guest and smashed glasses. Zelda, too, was becoming dangerously unpredictable. At the end of 1926, Scott was filled with self-disgust, and in the next few years, the couple tried to improve their lives.

But by 1929, Zelda was showing signs of mental disorder. In 1930, after several suicide attempts, she was admitted to

cess. As with Fitzgerald's own life, however, the dream leads to destruction. Carraway comes to despise the casual cruelty of the rich and famous, rather than envying their position and their wealth. And Gatsby realizes the emptiness and futility of his life.

a Swiss clinic. Between now and 1934, Zelda would have three breakdowns. The stress, combined with his alcoholism, took a toll on Scott's own health.

Still, Fitzgerald remained a dedicated professional in his work. He usually drafted his work in pencil, then typed, revised, and retyped it at least twice. After eight years and 17 drafts, *Tender is the Night* was published in 1934.

Soon after, Fitzgerald realized that Zelda would never get better. The lukewarm reception of his new book added to his misery, and he spent much of 1934 drunk, writing his wife sad letters.

ADMITTING DEFEAT

By now, Fitzgerald was a tired and sick 38-year-old. In 1936, *Esquire* magazine published a series of essays known as *The Crack-Up*, in which Scott admitted the waste of his life: "I have been a mediocre caretaker of the things left in my hands, even of my talent."

Fitzgerald's fortunes improved in 1937, when he was hired as a scriptwriter in Hollywood for a year. Relying heavily on the support of his new girlfriend, Sheila Graham, Fitzgerald battled against sickness and depression to complete *The Last Tycoon*.

Fitzgerald hoped that this book would reestablish him as the greatest American writer of his generation. But before he could complete it, he had a heart attack on Sunset Boulevard. One month later, on December 21, 1940, he collapsed with a second heart attack, and died shortly afterward, aged 44.

MAJOR WORKS	
1920	THIS SIDE OF PARADISE
1922	THE BEAUTIFUL AND THE DAMNED
1925	THE GREAT GATSBY
1934	TENDER IS THE NIGHT
1936	THE CRACK-UP

WILLIAM FAULKNER

One of the most innovative American novelists, William Faulkner combined a natural gift for storytelling with a bold, experimental style. In his works, he explored the darker aspects of life in his native Mississippi.

William Cuthbert Falkner was born on September 25, 1897, in New Albany, Mississippi, the first child of Murry and Maud Falkner—he added a "u" to his surname later in life. A year after his birth, the family moved to Ripley, where his father was an administrator of a railroad. They moved to Oxford, Mississippi, in 1902.

William was an avid reader and loved to sit listening to tales of the Old South. These early experiences led him to announce at the age of nine that he wanted to be a writer.

Around the age of ten, William became withdrawn and quiet. The townspeople thought he was odd, for he stood silently apart, watching them. He spent more time with his mother, and less with his three younger brothers. By the age of 13, he was writing poetry. He became further isolated from the people around him by wearing strange clothes.

In 1915, after twice failing to pass the 11th grade, he dropped out of school. His grandfather then gave him a job in his bank. He now began to drink, a habit he would have for the rest of his life.

As Faulkner's determination to be a writer grew, he found support in Phil Stone, a Yale graduate four years his senior. Stone read Faulkner's poetry and encouraged him. He also taught him Southern history, and introduced him to the work of great writers. Also crucial to Faulkner's development was his childhood sweetheart, Estelle Oldham. Faulkner trusted her and shared a great deal with her. When she married someone else in 1918, his world fell apart.

HUNGRY FOR ACTION

Seeking both an escape from his heartbreak and an occasion for heroism, Faulkner attempted to enlist in the army—the United States had entered World War I the year before—but he was rejected for being too short. He

William Faulkner, 1949
This photograph was taken in the year that Faulkner won the Nobel Prize for Literature—the high point of his literary career.

The Big Sleep: movie poster, 1946

In his final year working in Hollywood, Faulkner helped write the script of this highly successful movie, which was based on a detective novel by the writer Raymond Chandler.

tried again to enlist, this time in the British Royal Air Force, by claiming that he was English, and was accepted. Now calling himself "Faulkner," he attended flight school in Canada, but the war ended before he could see action. Returning home dejected, he invented tall stories about his war exploits, even pretending to have been wounded.

After the war, he returned to his poetry. In 1919, he had a poem published in *The New Republic* magazine. Five years later, his first book of poetry, *The Marble Faun*, appeared. He made ends

meet by working in a post office. He hated the job, and he was relieved when he was fired for incompetence.

A SWITCH TO PROSE

A turning point in Faulkner's career came in 1925, when he moved to New Orleans, and met Sherwood Anderson, a well-known writer. With Anderson's help, Faulkner started his first novel, *Soldier's Pay*. By the time it appeared in 1926, he was writing day and night. Soon he had published two more books: *Mosquitoes* in 1927, and *Sar-*

toris in 1929. *Sartoris* was the first of a series of novels set in the fictional Yoknapatawpha County, Mississippi, which bears a strong resemblance to the area of northern Mississippi where Faulkner spent most of his life.

With his next novel, *The Sound and the Fury*, Faulkner was finally recognized as a great talent. In the next decade, he wrote one work after another. These included *As I Lay Dying*—which he wrote in six weeks—*Light in August*, and *Absalom, Absalom!* All of his key themes—deterioration and death, racism, and the decline of the South—feature in these books. His work is marked by its groundbreaking style. By using flashbacks, repetition of phrases, several viewpoints of scenes, and Southern dialect, he makes his readers feel as if they live and feel the experiences and emotions of each character.

DECLINE AND COMEBACK

In 1929, Faulkner married Estelle, who had recently divorced. In 1930, they bought a house near Oxford, and the next year had a daughter. Although this was Faulkner's most creative period, money was short. Pressure to make money led him in 1931 to write *Sanctuary*, a violent novel that sold more than all of his other books combined. Lack of money also forced him to seek work in Hollywood. From 1932 to 1946, he worked on scripts for films such as *To Have and Have Not* and *The Big Sleep*. Faulkner detested this work and spent much of his time drinking.

Faulkner's career received a much-needed boost in 1944, when a critic named Malcolm Cowley wrote an essay reminding Americans of the genius in their midst. At the time, only one of Faulkner's 17 novels, *Sanctuary*, was still in print. Two years later, Cowley arranged with Faulkner to publish a selection of his work in *The Portable Faulkner*. The book revived the writer's reputation. In 1949, the renewed interest in Faulkner culminated in his winning the Nobel Prize for Literature. His literary eminence was assured, and the large cash prize relieved him once and for all of his money problems.

During the last decade of his life, Faulkner wrote two more novels, *A Fable* and *The Reivers*, both of which won Pulitzer Prizes. He also traveled on behalf of the State Department, promoting American literature. From 1957, he was writer-in-residence at the University of Virginia at Charlottesville, where he enjoyed his leisure time by hunting and drinking bourbon. Both hobbies took their toll. Weakened by a lifetime of alcoholic indulgence and several falls from horses, he died of a heart attack on July 6, 1962.

MAJOR WORKS

1929	SARTORIS; THE SOUND AND THE FURY
1930	AS I LAY DYING
1932	LIGHT IN AUGUST
1936	ABSALOM! ABSALOM!
1954	A FABLE
1962	THE REIVERS

ERNEST HEMINGWAY

A dedicated perfectionist in his writing, Hemingway wrote bold and passionate novels packed with action, violence, love, and death. His sharp, economical style was highly influential for generations of writers.

Ernest Miller Hemingway, the second of six children, was born on July 21, 1899, in Oak Park, Illinois, a wealthy suburb of Chicago. From his father, Dr. Clarence Hemingway, Ernest learned to love outdoor pursuits such as hunting and fishing. Ernest's mother, Grace, was sensitive and religious.

In high school, Hemingway read constantly. He had his first short stories published in the school magazine in 1916. After graduating in 1917, he joined the *Kansas City Star* newspaper as a junior reporter. He worked on the paper for seven months.

TO WAR

At this time, World War I was raging in Europe, and the young Hemingway longed to join the action. He volunteered twice but was rejected because of his weak eyesight. Then, in 1918, the Red Cross accepted him as a volunteer for the Italian Army. During a bombardment at the front, a fellow-soldier was injured, and Hemingway tried to carry him to safety. But he got caught in gunfire, which shattered his legs and body with hundreds of metal fragments.

Doctors managed to save Hemingway's legs, and the Italians awarded him a silver medal for bravery. While in the hospital, Hemingway fell in love with a nurse named Agnes. But she thought he was too young for her—he was not yet 20—and rejected him.

Shaken, Hemingway returned to Oak Park. Soon after, he moved on to Chicago. In 1920, he met Elizabeth Hadley Richardson, a talented pianist. They married in 1921 and moved to France. Settled in Paris, Ernest wrote a series of *Letters from Europe* for the *Toronto Star*. He spent much of his time in cafés, writing or talking to other writers. The Hemingways also visited Spain, where Ernest was thrilled by the bullfights. Their son, John Hadley Nicanor Hemingway, was born in October 1923.

Ernest Hemingway, 1944, by Kurt Hulton
Writer and war correspondent Hemingway types a report on World War II.

The family, living in a tiny Paris apartment, was quite poor. Eventually, however, Ernest got a job editing the *Transatlantic Review*, and gradually his future began to look brighter. Over the next two years, he published three novels, including *The Sun Also Rises* (1926). This sold well and was acclaimed by the critics.

SUCCESS AND CHANGE

By now Hemingway was a celebrity. The French magazine *Vogue* sent their fashion editor, Pauline Pfeiffer, to interview him. They fell in love, and after a short time, Hemingway asked Hadley for a divorce. On May 10, 1927, Ernest and Pauline were married.

The couple left Paris and moved to Key West, Florida. The writer now lived in style. He bought a yacht and spent his time fishing. But in 1928, tragedy struck when Hemingway's father shot himself. Ernest was devastated, describing his father as "a coward."

In the same year, he wrote *A Farewell to Arms*, describing the love between a wounded soldier and a nurse, which drew on his own experiences in Italy. Hemingway had great dedication to his work: "I rewrote the ending to *A Farewell to Arms*, the last page of it, 39 times before I was satisfied."

In search of adventure, he and Pauline went on a hunting expedition to Africa. He used his experiences of traveling and shooting big game to write some of his best short stories, including "The Snows of Kilimanjaro."

More success and fame followed. But the writer was still restless. When the

HEMINGWAY ON WRITING

A man with many passions, Hemingway's greatest love was writing. He had strong ideas about his art.

Hemingway's economic style is one of the striking characteristics of his work. This style stemmed partly from his early experience as a journalist. He believed that a writer should aim for clarity in his work, cutting out all extra detail. He felt that prose "should read easily and simply and seem short and yet have all the dimensions of the visible world and the world of a man's spirit."

Hemingway declared that it was vital for a writer to observe truthfully and record accurately. He felt that a writer's material had to come from personal experience, or else it would not be convincing. So that he could

Spanish Civil War broke out in 1936, Hemingway went to Spain immediately as a war correspondent. His experiences there inspired him to write *For Whom the Bell Tolls* in 1940.

Hemingway loved to write about war: "War groups the maximum of material and speeds up the action and brings out all sorts of stuff that normally you would have to wait a lifetime to

put this into practice, he carried a portable typewriter (*above*) with him wherever he went in case of inspiration. As he explained, "... whatever success I have had has been through writing what I know about."

Despite his love of writing, Hemingway often confessed that he did not find it easy. As he admitted to a critic in 1935: "Writing is something that you can never do as well as it can be done. It is a perpetual challenge and it is more difficult than anything else that I have ever done—so I do it. And it makes me happy when I do it well."

get." He also wrote about bullfighting, boxing, and other sports that tested an individual's courage and endurance.

Hemingway's fictional world is a violent one in which men struggle against difficult odds with little hope of victory. What mattered to him was how a man conducted himself during the struggle: His work celebrates the ability to show "grace under pressure."

Before Hemingway left for Spain in 1936, he had met Martha Gellhorn, a journalist. They met again in Spain. By 1940, Hemingway had left Pauline, married Martha, and set up home in Havana, Cuba.

When the United States entered World War II in 1941, Hemingway again became a war correspondent. Three years later, in London, Hemingway fell in love with another journalist, Mary Welsh. His relationship with Martha had ended, and he married Mary in 1946.

AN HONOR AND TRAGEDY

In 1954, the writer won the Nobel Prize for literature. By now, his health and eyesight were poor, and writing had become increasingly difficult. Worried that Cuba was on the verge of civil war, the Hemingways left the country, and settled near Ketchum, Idaho.

In old age, Hemingway was frail and depressed. He tried to kill himself several times, but Mary stopped him. Finally, in the early hours of July 2, 1961, the writer loaded a shotgun, and fired it into his mouth. The man who had boxed, skied, fished, hunted, and seen several wars, had killed himself.

MAJOR WORKS

1926	THE SUN ALSO RISES
1929	A FAREWELL TO ARMS
1932	DEATH IN THE AFTERNOON
1940	FOR WHOM THE BELL TOLLS

ZORA NEALE HURSTON

Hurston's depictions of the lives of African Americans made her the most widely published female black writer in the United States. But literary success did not bring financial security, and she died penniless.

Zora Neale Hurston was born in Notasulga, Alabama, probably in 1891. When she was very young, her family moved to Eatonville, Florida. This was the first all-black, self-governed town in the United States. It was a good place in which to grow up. According to Hurston, it had "five lakes, three croquet courts … plenty guavas, two schools, and no jail houses." Also, it provided shelter from the racism that many African Americans had to suffer in the South at the time.

Zora was a lively child, interested in everything around her. In particular, she enjoyed listening to neighbors telling old tales. Zora was close to her mother, Lucy, who urged her to "jump at the sun"—to strive for the best.

Zora's happiness came to an end when her mother died in 1904. Within two weeks, her father, John—a Baptist preacher and mayor of Eatonville—sent her away to live with her brother in Jacksonville, Florida. At first, she went to school. But after a while, she left to look after her brother's children. For the next few years, she had several jobs, including domestic servant, waitress, and manicurist. At one stage, she was maid to an actress in a touring theater group. For 18 months, Hurston traveled with the actors, feeling like part of their family. It was one of the happiest periods of her life.

THE START OF A CAREER

But she wanted to complete her high school education. By 1917, she had saved enough money for her tuition, and enrolled at the Morgan Academy in Baltimore, Maryland. She graduated in June 1918, and went on to Howard University in Washington, D.C.

There, Hurston began to write. In 1921, she had her first success when one of her stories appeared in the university's literary magazine.

Zora Neale Hurston
This undated photograph shows Hurston sometime in the 1950s. By this time, she was living back in Florida.

In January 1925, Hurston moved to New York. The city was experiencing a burst of African American creativity. Artists, writers, musicians, singers, and dancers were all part of a movement that became known as the Harlem Renaissance. This was named for the black community of Harlem, in which it was centered.

Hurston was inspired by all this artistic activity. She had a story appear in *Opportunity*, the leading magazine of black writing. The piece was based on her memories of Eatonville. In May 1925, she won two awards from the magazine—one for fiction and one for drama. One of the judges was the playwright Eugene O'Neill (*see page 52*).

The prizes brought Hurston to the attention of the Harlem Renaissance writers. She shared their aim of writing about African Americans and black folk culture. She was soon accepted into their circle, earning the nickname "Queen of the Harlem Renaissance."

At the same time, she enrolled at Barnard College, becoming the college's first black student. She took a course in cultural anthropology, the study of peoples' traditions, customs, and lifestyles. She later continued her studies at Columbia University.

TRAVELS AND SUCCESS

In 1927, she married Herbert Sheen, an old flame from Howard University, but they divorced four years later. One of the reasons the marriage broke down was that Hurston was often traveling. In the late 1920s and 1930s, she made several research trips back to her

THE HARLEM RENAISSANCE

In the 1920s, Harlem was the center of a major flowering of art, literature, and music.

In 1921, the first major black musical, *Shuffle Along*, opened on Broadway. It marked the start of a decade of intense artistic creativity among the African American community in Harlem. During this period, black writers created more works and received more acclaim than ever before, black musicians played to packed houses, and black artists enjoyed unprecedented success.

Although the movement included a variety of art forms and styles, most artists and writers aimed to portray the everyday lives and experiences of African Americans. Many wanted to use their skills to fight the evils of

Southern homeland, gathering material on African American life. She also made trips to the Caribbean. Wherever she went, she asked questions and took notes. People liked and accepted her, speaking freely, even about such secret matters as voodoo—ancient religious and magical practices.

From the early 1930s, Hurston published the results of her studies in nov-

racism, and to bring whites and blacks together. To a degree, it worked. Suddenly, black culture was in fashion. For the first time, many white people read the work of black writers, such as Hurston, Langston Hughes, and Alain Locke. They also flocked to Harlem to enjoy the music and dancing in jazz clubs, including the Cotton Club, where Cab Calloway (*above*) and Duke Ellington played with their bands.

els such as her masterpiece, *Their Eyes Were Watching God,* and in a number of folklore books, including *Mules and Men* and *Tell My Horse.* She also wrote many articles, plays, and an autobiography, *Dust Tracks on the Road.* In all her works, she painted a vivid picture of black culture in the Deep South, recording her own past and the lives and customs of the peo-

ple she had met. She celebrated their habits, the way they spoke and sang, and the things they laughed at. Her fiction, journalism, and cultural research made her the most productive black woman writer in the United States.

Even so, she earned little from her writing. Some Harlem Renaissance writers now criticized her for showing only the good side of black life. They accused her of ignoring the misery of racism. They also attacked her use of black dialect, which they thought was too similar to racist impersonations of African American speech.

YEARS OF POVERTY

Although she continued to write in the late 1940s, Hurston found it increasingly difficult to get her work published. She was always very short of money. In 1949, she moved back to Florida, where she worked first as a maid, then as a librarian and a teacher. Ten years later, she had a stroke, and moved into the county welfare home. On January 28, 1960, she died at the age of 69. Penniless, she was buried in an unmarked grave.

MAJOR WORKS

1935	MULES AND MEN
1937	THEIR EYES WERE WATCHING GOD
1938	TELL MY HORSE
1939	MOSES, MAN OF THE MOUNTAIN
1942	DUST TRACKS ON A ROAD

JOHN STEINBECK

A shy, modest man who shunned fame and publicity, Steinbeck devoted himself to his work. In his novels, he championed the cause of the poor and oppressed, creating powerful fiction that won him literature's highest honors.

John Ernst Steinbeck was born on February 27, 1902, in Salinas, California. He was something of a loner, and found it difficult to mix socially. A day-dreamer with a gift for telling stories, he decided early on to become a writer.

From 1919 to 1925, he studied at Stanford University. During vacations, he worked on ranches and farms, and in factories. The appalling working conditions and pitiful wages in these jobs made him very angry.

Steinbeck left Stanford determined to write, but his first job as a reporter in New York was unsuccessful. He was fired from the *New York American* for incompetence. He returned to California, and worked as a caretaker. This gave him time to write, and between 1929 and 1933, he published three novels. They attracted little attention.

During this period, he formed a close friendship with Ed Ricketts, a marine biologist. Ricketts was a serious man who enjoyed philosophical discussion. The two men talked about Steinbeck's view that humans were animals like any other, with the same primitive instincts and impulses as lower species. In *The Sea of Cortez*, an account of a research voyage he took with Ricketts, he wrote: "There would seem to be only one commandment for living things: Survive!"

MARRIAGE AND SUCCESS

In 1930, Steinbeck had married Carol Henning. For five years, they lived in poverty. Then, in 1935, the appearance of *Tortilla Flat* brought success at last. The book told the tale of a band of poor but happy *paisanos*—Mexican Californians—who spend their days philosophizing and drifting. Despite a mixed critical reaction, the book was a best-seller, and Steinbeck received $4,000 for the movie rights. Success also brought fame. But Steinbeck shunned this, regarding it as "a pain."

John Steinbeck, 1962
In 1962, the 60-year-old Steinbeck won the Nobel Prize for Literature. This photograph was taken to mark the occasion.

He now threw himself into his work. *In Dubious Battle*, published in 1936, concerned a Communist-led strike by migrant workers. The novel aroused the suspicions of some politicians who suspected the writer of sympathizing with communism. The next year, *Of Mice and Men* was also a best-seller. It deals with two drifting farmhands whose ambition to own a small piece of land is shattered when one of them accidentally kills a woman.

YEARS OF SUCCESS

Two years later, in 1939, *The Grapes of Wrath* appeared. The tale relates the journey of the Joad family from the Oklahoma Dust Bowl to the fertile farms of California, and their battles with greedy landowners. Their trip turns into a struggle for survival. It is a metaphor for the strength of the human spirit.

The novel stunned America, and sparked a fierce debate about whether it was art or propaganda. Steinbeck was again accused of spreading Communist ideas. Some libraries burned copies of the book, the Kansas City Board of Education banned it, and Congressman Lyle Boren of Oklahoma called it "a lie, a black, infernal creation of a twisted, distorted mind." Nevertheless, it became a best-seller, and won Steinbeck the Pulitzer Prize in 1940.

Steinbeck was now wealthy: Four of his novels had been filmed in as many years. But his marriage was failing. He fell in love with Gwendolyn Conger, a singer, and married her in 1943.

When the United States entered World War II, Steinbeck supported the

THE GRAPES OF WRATH

Steinbeck's powerful and complex tale of one family's long journey west is now considered his masterpiece.

In 1938, Steinbeck visited the camps of migrants who traveled from drought-stricken Oklahoma to find work in California. When he saw the thousands of starving people, he had to speak out.

The result was *The Grapes of Wrath*, the tale of a family of Oklahoma tenant farmers, the Joads. When drought comes and the crop fails, they are evicted from their farm. With their last dollars, they buy an old truck and set off for the lush greenery of California—the "promised land." On the way, they suffer severe hardship, only to discover when they arrive that "It ain't no lan' of milk and honey."

war effort. He could not join the army, however, because of his alleged Communist sympathies. Instead, he wrote morale-boosting work, such as *The Moon is Down*, a novel based on the Nazi occupation of Norway. During 1943, he was war reporter for the *New York Herald Tribune*. He traveled to North Africa, and went to Italy with the Allied invasion.

Ma Joad (*above left*) is typical of Steinbeck's heroic figures. She is the heart of the family, and her determination to survive drives the others on. By contrast, Pa Joad (*above right*) becomes confused, uncertain, and lost when deprived of his work.

When the novel appeared, it caused a storm. Those whom the book attacked, such as heartless landowners, bankers, and politicians, claimed that it was all lies. But thousands of "Okies" who had made the same journey as the Joads knew without a doubt that it was true. It was their own tragic story.

Steinbeck spent part of the postwar years traveling in Europe. On his return, Gwendolyn asked for a divorce. Their marriage had become increasingly strained, and she confessed to having an affair. Steinbeck's misery deepened when Ed Ricketts was killed in a car accident. After a period of drinking and womanizing back in California, Steinbeck met Elaine Scott, whom he married in 1950. He said: "It is the first peace I have had with a woman."

During the 1950s, Steinbeck turned increasingly to journalism, although he continued to write fiction, including *East of Eden*. This reworking of the Bible story of Cain and Abel became a movie starring James Dean. His books continued to be popular, but some critics accused him of sentimentality. He also shocked many people with his support of the war in Vietnam, for which some Americans never forgave him. Although indifferent to praise, Steinbeck was hurt by criticism, and he considered retiring.

LATE HONOR

His greatest honor was still to come, however. In 1962, he received the Nobel Prize for Literature. He felt honored, but was typically modest. When a reporter asked him if he felt he deserved the prize, he replied: "Frankly, no."

On December 20, 1968, after some months of ill-health, Steinbeck died in New York of heart failure. He was 66. Shortly after, Elaine and Steinbeck's son, Thom, took his ashes to California and buried them.

MAJOR WORKS

1935	TORTILLA FLAT
1936	IN DUBIOUS BATTLE
1937	OF MICE AND MEN
1939	THE GRAPES OF WRATH
1952	EAST OF EDEN

CHARLES IVES

After years of musical obscurity, Ives is now regarded as one of the truly great American composers. Fiercely original, Ives ignored his critics and challenged contemporary ideas of music in a highly influential way.

Charles Edward Ives was born in Danbury, Connecticut, on October 20, 1874. His father, George Ives, was a musician who conducted bands and choirs, and also taught music theory. As a boy, Charles took music lessons from his father. By the age of 14, he had a job as a church organist, and had begun to write his own music. Charles was not only musically talented: He also excelled in baseball and football.

A MUSICAL RADICAL

Ives's musical influences included traditional types of American music, such as hymns and marches. But modern ideas also inspired him. Ives's father experimented, challenging traditional ideas about music—including the idea that dissonant sounds had to resolve to more stable ones. He would make the young Charles sing in one key while accompanying him on the piano in a different key, creating a clashing of tones.

Ives later recalled how his father dismissed the classical idea that dis-

sonant sounds—those which are restless, and jarring to the ear—always had to resolve to stable ones. George Ives insisted: "Every dissonance doesn't have to resolve if it doesn't happen to feel like it, any more than every horse should have to have its tail bobbed just because it's the prevailing fashion."

In 1894, the 20-year-old Ives entered Yale University, where he studied composition with Horatio Parker, a well-known composer. While at Yale, Ives could not write music that was too radical if he hoped to pass his courses. For this reason, his First Symphony, completed in 1898, sounds more conservative than much of his later music.

When he graduated from Yale in 1898, Ives decided not to follow a career in music. He knew that only a very few people would support the kind of music he wanted to write. Instead, he chose to go into the insurance business,

Charles Ives, 1950, by Eugene Smith
This publicity photograph shows the composer at the age of 76.

Concert in Central Park, New York, 1930s

In *Central Park in the Dark*, Ives tried to evoke an image of the city as heard from the park—the sounds of horses' hooves, people talking, and pianos playing ragtime music.

where he made his fortune. This financial security gave him the freedom to write any kind of music he wanted. He composed in the evenings and on weekends, writing symphonies, songs, choral works, and piano pieces.

During the first years of the 20th century, Ives produced several experimental pieces. His desire to embody in music the sounds that he heard around him inspired most of these. If life contained dissonance, he believed, then so should music.

This approach is illustrated in one of Ives's best-known works, *Central Park*

in the Dark (1906). Ives described the work as an evocation of "the sounds of nature and happenings that men would hear some 30 years ago … when sitting on a bench in Central Park on a hot summer night." Among the sounds he captures are fire trucks, a runaway horse, and the cries of newsboys.

Most of Ives's music would not be performed until many years after he wrote it: Performers were reluctant to risk playing music that their audiences would not like. But this lack of recognition did not bother Ives. He was committed to his own musical vision.

One person who supported his music was Harmony Twichell, whom he met in 1905 and married three years later. She was unflinching in her encouragement of her husband, even when his own resolve faltered.

Throughout his works, Ives combined elements of the music that surrounded him—such as hymns, marches, folk music, jazz, and patriotic music—with modern compositional techniques. In his orchestral work, *The Fourth of July* (1913), for example, he gives his impression of watching festivities in a New England town. At one point, the listener hears two marching bands approaching from opposite directions. Each band is playing a different tune in a different key, so that the music eventually dissolves into clashing dissonance and broken rhythms.

A SPIRITUAL INSPIRATION

Ives also found inspiration beyond the everyday world. He was interested in Transcendentalism, a philosophy that emphasized the spiritual aspects of man and nature. The ideas of the main thinkers in this movement, "The Concord Four"—writers Ralph Waldo Emerson, Nathaniel Hawthorne, Henry David Thoreau, and Bronson Alcott—gradually filtered into much of Ives's work. The most famous example of this influence is the *Concord* Sonata for piano (1911-1915). Ives described this piece as "one person's impression of the spirit of Transcendentalism."

Ives composed steadily until 1918, when he had a heart attack. After that, his activities as a composer came to a

virtual standstill. But now the music he had already written increasingly began to attract attention. Ives published his *Concord* Sonata in 1920, together with a collection of essays outlining his artistic philosophies. These *Essays Before a Sonata*, as he called them, sparked the first genuine interest in Ives's work.

In the 1930s, the American conductor Nicolas Slonimsky premiered several of Ives's orchestral works. At first, audiences were hostile. When one performance broke down into chaos, the composer was thrilled, remarking, "Just like a town meeting—every man for himself. Wonderful how it came out!"

In spite of their initial incomprehension, audiences and critics slowly began to warm to Ives's music. In 1945, he was elected to the National Institute of Arts and Letters. Two years later, he was awarded the Pulitzer Prize for his Third Symphony.

Ives had a stroke while recuperating from a minor operation. He died on May 19, 1954, in New York. Since his death, Ives has become recognized as one of America's most original composers.

MAJOR WORKS

1898	FIRST SYMPHONY
1906	CENTRAL PARK IN THE DARK
1911-15	CONCORD SONATA
1913	THE FOURTH OF JULY
1922	114 SONGS

IGOR STRAVINSKY

Igor Stravinsky shocked the musical world with his startling compositions. The Russian-born composer's daring and dynamic work broke with the traditions of the past, and led music into the modern world.

Igor Stravinsky was born near St. Petersburg, Russia, on June 17, 1882. His father was an opera singer, and his mother was a fine pianist. At nine, Stravinsky began to study music. He especially loved to improvise his own piano pieces. He made few friends at school, but his passion for music helped cure his loneliness.

A CELEBRATED MENTOR

In 1901, Stravinsky followed his parents' advice and enrolled in St. Petersburg University to study law. He could not forget music, however, and before long he was composing seriously. In 1902, he met the famous Russian composer Nikolai Rimsky-Korsakov. Rimsky-Korsakov recognized his talent, and took him on as a pupil. They became very close: Rimsky-Korsakov was like a father to the young man, particularly after Stravinsky's real father died in 1902.

Stravinsky left the university in 1905 without graduating. A year later, he married his cousin, Katerina Nossenko.

The couple would have a son and a daughter within two years.

In the summer of 1908, Stravinsky completed his first major work, an orchestral fantasy called *Fireworks*, which was premiered in St. Petersburg the following year. Among those in the audience was Sergei Diaghilev, the director of a famous dance company, the Ballets Russes. On hearing *Fireworks*, he invited Stravinsky to come to Paris, where his company was enjoying phenomenal success.

For his first season with the Ballets Russes, Stravinsky orchestrated other composers' music. In 1909, however, Diaghilev asked him to write a ballet based on a Russian legend of a bird that rises from the ashes of a fire. The result was *The Firebird*. When the new ballet premiered in Paris the following year, the audience greeted it ecstatically.

Igor Stravinsky, 1956
This picture shows the 76-year-old composer in St. Mark's Square in Venice, Italy. He would eventually be buried in the city.

In 1911, Stravinsky had an even greater success with his next ballet, *Petrushka*—the story of a puppet clown who survives murder to taunt and jeer the audience. In this work, he used polytonality—the use of two or more keys at once—for the first time.

A CONTROVERSIAL WORK

Around this period, Stravinsky began to write a ballet based on ancient pagan rituals celebrating the arrival of spring. Stravinsky wanted to evoke the powerful forces of nature and the most primitive of human instincts. To do this, he broke completely with musical tradition, and used strange sounds and irregular rhythms that jarred the ear.

When the work, *The Rite of Spring*, was premiered in May 1913, it was one of the musical events of the century. Both the music and the dancing offended many in the audience—the music was highly dissonant, while the dancing was provocative. People showed their anger by rioting in the theater.

YEARS OF TRAVEL

When World War I broke out in 1914, Stravinsky and his family moved to Switzerland. He now became obsessed with his native Russia, and a stream of Russian-inspired works followed. These included *The Soldier's Tale*, based on a Russian folktale, and *Mavra*, a comic opera based on a story by the Russian writer Aleksander Pushkin.

In 1920, Stravinsky returned to France. He now spent most of his time traveling. In 1921, he visited Spain, England, and the United States. He had

THE RITE OF SPRING

On May 29, 1913, Stravinsky's ballet, *The Rite of Spring* premiered in Paris. It caused a sensation.

The first showing of Stravinsky's ballet caused an explosive reaction. No one had ever heard music like this before. It seemed to reject the harmony, tone, and expression in music that people were used to. To many, *The Rite of Spring* sounded savage, brutal, and chaotic.

It was not only the music that caused an uproar. The dancing for the ballet was planned by the famous Russian dancer, Vaslav Nijinsky. His revolutionary choreography consisted largely of complex, awkward movements. A series of contemporary sketches (*above right*) suggest some of these twists and turns.

little time to devote to the Ballets Russes, and after *Pulcinella* in 1920, he wrote no more works for them. Diaghilev was angry to lose him, and their friendship came to an end. There was little time to heal the rift: In August 1929, Diaghilev died in Venice, Italy.

In 1934, Stravinsky became a French citizen. His future lay not in Europe, however, but in America, where his

The audience was stunned. Catcalls rang out through the theater, and fights broke out between excited artists and students, and traditionalists. Stravinsky's ballet had shattered the barriers of music and dance, and introduced a forceful and influential new approach.

music was increasingly successful. In 1935, he toured the United States, and received several commissions. They came at a low point in Stravinsky's life: His daughter, wife, and mother had all died within months of each other from tuberculosis. The composer overcame his grief by throwing himself into his work. In 1939, he married Vera de Bosset, an actress and old friend.

That year, he made the United States his permanent home, eventually settling in Hollywood. He became a U.S. citizen in 1945. He devoted the next three years of his life to writing a full-length opera.

The new work was inspired by *A Rake's Progress*, a set of engravings by the 18th-century English artist William Hogarth that show a rich young man wasting his inheritance. Stravinsky conducted the premiere in 1951, which was yet another great success.

In later life, the composer toured America and Europe. In 1962, he made a triumphant return to Russia after nearly 50 years' absence. He received a hero's welcome: 30,000 people stood in line for his concerts in his home city of St. Petersburg—then Leningrad—and the Soviet leader, Nikita Khruschev, gave him a reception in the Kremlin.

By 1967, the composer's health was failing: He had suffered from tuberculosis for many years. On April 6, 1971, at the age of 88, he died at his New York home. He was buried in Venice, near Diaghilev's grave.

MAJOR WORKS

1910	THE FIREBIRD
1911	PETRUSHKA
1913	THE RITE OF SPRING
1918	THE SOLDIER'S TALE
1920	PULCINELLA
1927	OEDIPUS REX
1951	THE RAKE'S PROGRESS

GEORGE GERSHWIN

Gershwin's career is a typical "rags-to-riches" story. Brought up in one of the poorest areas of New York, the composer went on to become a national celebrity with his popular songs and innovative, jazz-inspired symphonies.

George Gershwin was born on September 26, 1898. His parents, Rosa and Moishe Gershovitz, were Russian Jewish immigrants who had come to the United States in 1891. They settled in Brooklyn, New York, and Americanized their name to Gershwin.

In 1910, the Gershwins bought a piano for their eldest son, Israel, or Ira. But it was George who started to play. He had an exceptional talent, and his parents decided to find him a music teacher. He made great progress, and in 1914, at the age of 15, he decided to leave accounting school to pursue a career in music.

He became a "song plugger," promoting songs for a publisher on Tin Pan Alley—the center of popular music. For a salary of $15 a week, Gershwin played the piano in a booth to demonstrate his company's songs to buyers. Although it was hard work, he enjoyed it. But his ambition was to get his own songs published. He did not have to wait long: He offered his music for sale around Tin Pan Alley, and eventually had his first work published in 1917.

Two years later, he wrote his first complete Broadway score, *La La Lucille,* and had his first hit song, "Swanee," which Al Jolson made famous in the show *Sinbad.* Over the next few years, his work went from strength to strength, and he became an established Broadway songwriter.

INFLUENCE OF JAZZ

At this time, jazz was sweeping the nation. Its exciting rhythms and infectious melodies were having a huge impact on other forms of music. Gershwin himself wrote several jazz-inspired songs before attempting a large-scale "jazz concerto" in 1924. The composition, *Rhapsody in Blue,* was one of the first to combine the controversial techniques of jazz with those of classical

George Gershwin, 1928
Gershwin, by now a sought-after star, poses for a photograph that was used to advertise the famous Steinway piano company.

Scene from An American in Paris, *1951*
Popular singer and dancer Gene Kelly starred in this successful Hollywood movie. The lively score, first performed in 1928, is one of Gershwin's most popular.

music, which was considered more "respectable." It was an overwhelming success and marked Gershwin's arrival as a serious composer. He repeated this triumph the next year, with a similar work, Concerto in F.

FRUITFUL PARTNERSHIP

Between *Rhapsody in Blue* and the Concerto in F, Gershwin had created another Broadway hit, *Lady, Be Good!* The show starred Fred and Adele Astaire as a brother and sister act. It was also the first major collaboration between George, who wrote the music, and his brother Ira, who wrote the

words. Although they were complete opposites—George was bouncy and friendly, Ira was quiet and shy—they made a perfect team. From 1925 until 1933, they enjoyed repeated triumphs on the Broadway stage, including *Funny Face* in 1927 and *Rosalie* in 1928. Thanks to these successes, Gershwin was able to buy a large house. He could also afford expensive hobbies, including collecting modern art.

In 1928, Gershwin took a trip to Europe. While in Paris, he sketched out an orchestral composition. Later that year, he premiered the work, *An American in Paris*, at Carnegie Hall. It confirmed his status as the young leader of new American music.

Hollywood was the next goal. In 1931, George and Ira made their debut there with the score for the movie, *Delicious*. After returning to New York, George wrote the Second Rhapsody for Orchestra with Piano, another success.

REPEATED FAILURES

The Great Depression had little effect on Gershwin's career. He had plenty of money, and was enjoying hit after hit. In 1933, however, he and Ira wrote the songs for *Pardon My English*. The show was a flop. At the time, this did not seem to affect George, but then his next show, *Let 'Em Eat Cake*, also flopped. Although these two disasters did not put him into financial difficulties, they did affect his mental state. He now underwent psychoanalysis.

The next year, Gershwin set off on a grueling 12,000-mile concert tour with a 50-piece orchestra. It took him to 40 cities in the United States and Canada. Upon his return, he started work on his only opera, *Porgy and Bess*. This was based on DuBose Heyward's novel, *Porgy*, which Gershwin had read in 1926. For this project, he needed a sustained effort. He gave up all his luxuries and comforts for two months, and went into retreat with Ira and Heyward to work.

The isolation paid off, and by the fall of 1934, Gershwin had drafted most of the opera. He completed it just in time for the opening on Broadway in October 1935. Although this mixture of opera and musical comedy would later become one of Gershwin's most popu-

lar works, at the time it aroused criticism. It was his third flop in a row. He now looked west again, and after a last performance in New York in July 1936, he returned to Hollywood with Ira.

RETURN TO HOLLYWOOD

The Gershwins' second stay in Tinseltown was an artistic and financial success. They wrote the scores for two Fred Astaire movies, *Shall We Dance?* and *A Damsel in Distress* in 1937. George also enjoyed a hectic social life: He had affairs with many women, including the French actress, Simone Simon, and Paulette Goddard, wife of movie star Charlie Chaplin.

In June 1937, the normally healthy Gershwin experienced dizziness and headaches, which he put down to overwork. He rejected the idea of being examined by a doctor. It was a foolish mistake: He fell into a coma, and doctors discovered a brain tumor. On July 11, 1937, he had an emergency operation, but died five hours later without regaining consciousness. He was just 39. Americans felt his loss deeply. He was given two huge funerals, one in New York and the other in Hollywood.

MAJOR WORKS

1924	RHAPSODY IN BLUE
1925	CONCERTO IN F
1926	PIANO PRELUDES
1928	AN AMERICAN IN PARIS
1934-35	PORGY AND BESS

AARON COPLAND

Probably the United States most popular composer of concert music, Copland created a sound that was unmistakably American. During his glittering career, he won critical acclaim, musical awards, and national honors.

Aaron Copland was born in Brooklyn, New York, on November 14, 1900. There were five children in the Copland household—three boys and two girls. Aaron was the youngest.

Like all his brothers and sisters, he took music lessons as a child. No one expected him to have a career in music, however. But when he was 15, he decided to become a composer. After some persuasion, his parents agreed to let him study music seriously.

From 1917, he studied with the well-known American composer, Rubin Goldmark. Goldmark's tastes in music were conservative. By contrast, his student was interested in "radical" modern composers who shocked their audiences with strange new musical sounds.

In 1921, Copland applied to a new music school for Americans near Paris, France. He was accepted. During his three years there, he studied with the great French teacher, Nadia Boulanger.

He now started to compose. Boulanger urged him to experiment. She told him: "To study music, we must learn the rules. To create music, we must forget them." With her encouragement, in 1923 Copland began to write his first large-scale work, the Symphony for Organ and Orchestra. He said that he wanted to produce a piece that would "immediately be recognized as American in character." To achieve this, he introduced elements of jazz, America's new form of popular music.

SHOCKING THE PUBLIC

Copland returned to the United States in June 1924, and his new piece was premiered the next year. The symphony's modern sound and jazzy melodies and rhythms shocked many people in the audience. Everyone agreed, however, that a great young talent had arrived. Copland quickly followed this work with several more, including

Aaron Copland
This photograph, which was taken in the late 1930s, shows Copland as he works on a new composition.

Music for the Theater in 1925, and the Piano Concerto in 1927.

Copland was soon winning widespread recognition. In 1927, he became the first composer to win a Guggenheim Fellowship. Two years later, he won a $5,000 prize for his *Dance* Symphony.

PROMOTER OF NEW MUSIC

In 1928, he organized a series of concerts to promote new American music. This was his first of many efforts to encourage homegrown talent. In 1932, he became the first director of the Festival of Contemporary Music at Yaddo, near Sarasota Springs, New York, and, in 1937, he was elected president of the American Composers Alliance.

Copland was also interested in teaching. He wanted people to understand his style of music. He taught a course in modern music at the New School for Social Research in New York from 1927 to 1937. Later in life, he lectured at a number of other institutions as well. He also wrote several books on music. To help young people get involved in music, he wrote several works for performance in schools.

A NEW STYLE

In 1930, Copland changed his style. He now began to write more complex pieces. These included the Piano Variations and the *Short* Symphony, both of which earned him respect from his musical colleagues. But after a while, Copland realized that his music had become "difficult to perform and difficult for an audience to comprehend." He felt that it was pointless to write

MUSIC FOR THE MOVIES

Copland was one of several famous concert composers who had successful careers in Hollywood.

Music has always been an important part of the movie experience. Silent films needed music to block out the noise of the film projectors and to highlight key moments of the stories. But the earliest movies did not have sound tracks. Instead, musicians played live music in the theater.

The invention of "talking pictures" in the 1920s made live performances unnecessary. Alfred Hitchcock's 1929 film *Blackmail* was the first to have a musical score synchronized with the film. One of the most famous Hollywood film composers was Max Steiner, who

music no one wanted to hear. He wanted people to enjoy his work.

In the late 1930s and 1940s, he wrote pieces in a simpler style. These included *El Salón México*, the ballets *Billy the Kid* and *Appalachian Spring*, *A Lincoln Portrait* for speaker and orchestra, and *Fanfare for the Common Man*. These works made him the most popular American composer of the

wrote the music for about 300 films during the 1930s and 40s, including *Gone with the Wind*.

Although Aaron Copland is best known for his concert works, he also wrote music for movies. His score for *The Heiress* (above) won him an Oscar in 1950. He wrote: "Film music makes sense only if it helps the film. No matter how good, ... or successful, the music must be secondary in importance to the story being told on the screen."

day. He also produced music for movies, writing scores for eight films, including *Of Mice and Men* and *The Red Pony*, both based on stories by John Steinbeck (*see page 72*).

Copland's music was becoming increasingly accessible, through his use of American subjects for his works. *A Lincoln Portrait*, for example, is about President Abraham Lin-

coln; *Billy the Kid* is about the legendary Wild West outlaw. He also used melodies from traditional American folk music. The best-known example of this is *Appalachian Spring*, for which he won both the Pulitzer Prize and the New York Critics' Circle award in 1945.

LATER YEARS

Copland continued to receive honors right up until his death. In 1964, President Lyndon B. Johnson awarded the composer the Presidential Medal of Freedom, the highest peacetime civilian honor. Copland also received honorary degrees from Harvard, Princeton, and other universities.

In the last decades of his life, Copland turned his attention away from composing toward conducting. He also remained a much loved and respected spokesman for American music. He died peacefully on December 12, 1990.

MAJOR WORKS

1923-24	SYMPHONY FOR ORGAN AND ORCHESTRA
1930	PIANO VARIATIONS
1933	SHORT SYMPHONY
1936	EL SALÓN MÉXICO
1938	BILLY THE KID
1942	A LINCOLN PORTRAIT; FANFARE FOR THE COMMON MAN
1944	APPALACHIAN SPRING

GLOSSARY

abstract art Art that does not represent objects or people that can be recognized in the real world, but that expresses a thought, idea, or feeling through colors and shapes.

academic art A traditional way of painting based on the art of the past.

avant-garde French for "advanced guard," a term describing artists and movements that are considered new, radical, or revolutionary.

collage From the French word meaning to stick, or glue; a picture built up by gluing pieces of paper, cloth, or other material to a surface.

commission An order received by an artist, writer, or composer from a patron to produce a work of art, literature, or music.

composition The arrangement or organization of the various elements of a work of art, literature, or music.

Cubism A style of art pioneered by Pablo Picasso and Georges Braque in the first decade of the 20th century. The Cubists rejected the idea that art must copy nature. They depicted the world as the mind knows it to be rather than as the eye sees it. For this reason, they often showed objects from several viewpoints at the same time.

Expressionism An early 20th-century movement in art that used strong colors and simple forms to express feelings and emotions.

Fauvism An early 20th-century style of art that emphasized strong colors and vigorous brushstrokes. The term comes from the French word *fauve* meaning "wild beast."

fiction A type of literature, such as novels and short stories, in which the characters and events are invented.

folklore The traditional beliefs, customs, and superstitions of a people that are handed down in myths, legends, and other fables.

Great Depression A period of high unemployment and economic misery that struck the United States after the stock market crash of October 1929.

Harlem Renaissance The time of intense artistic activity that took place in the African American New York district of Harlem in the 1920s.

improvisation A musical performance that is invented on the spur of the moment rather than planned and written beforehand.

jazz A kind of music that developed among the African American community at the end of the 19th century and grew in popularity during the 20th century.

Jazz Age A term used to describe the 1920s in the U. S., named for the new style of music that was sweeping the country. Also known as the Roaring Twenties, the postwar era was characterized by economic prosperity, Prohibition—the banning of the manufacture or sale of alcohol—and changes in American culture.

melodrama A sensational or extravagant work of drama. Often based on romantic novels or shocking crime stories, melodramas have thrilling plots and straightforward characters that appeal to the emotions.

modernism Modern artistic, musical, or literary practice that rejects the past for new forms of expression.

monologue A dramatic sketch or speech performed by a single actor.

mural A painting on a wall or ceiling.

novel An invented story that is usually long and complex, and deals especially with human experience.

ode A rhymed lyric poem, often in the form of an address, generally dignified in subject, feeling, and style.

opera A dramatic musical work in which the characters sing the text, accompanied by an orchestra.

patron A person or organization that asks an artist, writer, or composer to create a work of art, literature, or music. Usually, the patron pays for the work.

portrait A drawing, painting, photograph, or sculpture that gives a likeness of a person and often provides an insight into his or her personality.

print A picture produced by pressing a piece of paper against a variety of inked surfaces, including engraved metal plates and wooden blocks. There are several methods of making prints, such as engraving, etching, and lithography.

Romanticism An early 19th-century European and American movement in art, literature, and music that emphasized the free expression of emotion and imagination, passion, love of nature and exotic places, individual liberty, and social reform.

Salon The official, and most important, state art exhibit of France, held in the Louvre Museum in Paris.

style The distinctive appearance of a particular artist, writer, or composer's work of art.

symbol An object that represents something else; for example, a dove commonly symbolizes peace.

technique The way an artist uses his or her materials.

FURTHER READING

Bober, Natalie S. *A Restless Spirit: The Story of Robert Frost.* H. Holt & Co., 1991

Bosco, Peter. *World War I.* Facts on File, 1991

Farrell, Jacqueline. *The Great Depression.* Lucent Books, 1996

Janson, H.W. *The History of Art.* Abrams, 1995 (standard reference)

Kostenevich, A.G. and Frankel, Lory. *Henri Matisse.* Abrams, 1997

Metropolitan Museum of Art. *What Makes a Picasso a Picasso?* Muhlberger, Richard, text. Viking Children's Books, 1994

Neimark, Anne E. *Diego Rivera, Artist of the People.* HarperCollins Children's, 1992

The New Grove Dictionary of Music and Musicians. Grove's Dictionaries of Music, 1980 (standard reference)

Popov, Nicolai. *Stravinsky.* Creative Education, 1993

Ridley, Pauline. *Modern Art.* Thomson Learning, 1995

Seymour, Gene. *Jazz: The Great American Art.* Franklin Watts, 1995

Venezia, Mike. *George Gershwin.* Children's Press, 1994

Verde, Tom. *Twentieth-Century Writers: 1900-1950.* Facts on File, 1993

Witcover, Paul. *Zora Neale Hurston: Author.* Chelsea House, 1992

INDEX